# *Curious*
# COTSWOLDS

R.ᵉ WESTMACOTT Fecit 1791.

In the Memory of
JAMES LENOX DUTTON Esq.

# *Curious*
# COTSWOLDS

MARK TURNER

TEMPUS

*For Mum and Dad*

Frontispiece: *Westmacott's monument to James Lenox Dutton in Sherborne Church.*

First published 2006

Tempus Publishing Limited
The Mill, Brimscombe Port,
Stroud, Gloucestershire, GL5 2QG
www.tempus-publishing.com

© Mark Turner, 2006

The right of Mark Turner to be identified as the Author
of this work has been asserted in accordance with the
Copyrights, Designs and Patents Act 1988.

British Library Cataloguing in Publication Data.
A catalogue record for this book is available from the British Library.

ISBN 0 7524 3930 8

Typesetting and origination by Tempus Publishing Limited
Printed in Great Britain

# CONTENTS

# IMPORTANT NOTE

Many of the places of interest described in this book are accessible by public road or footpath and may be visited at any reasonable time. Some, however, are in private ownership and on private property. Permission should be sought from the owner before any attempt is made to visit such places. Entry to property without permission is, of course, trespass, and readers are advised to observe the law. Where permission to visit is received, readers are asked to show respect and consideration for property and persons.

It will be seen that a number of the locations described are in relatively remote situations. Vehicles left in such places are sometimes subject to the attentions of opportunist thieves. Readers are urged, therefore, not to leave any items of value – such as cameras, bags and expensive clothing – where they can be seen.

# INTRODUCTION

I've been curious for as long as I can remember. As a youngster in the Welsh border town of Monmouth, I was more interested in ancient burial mounds than football and I preferred chatting with elderly antiquarians than with grinning schoolgirls. But that isn't to say I was a prude. When only fifteen I'd worked out which pub landlord wasn't too fussy about the age of his customers, and I was more than happy to spend hours hanging out in smoke-filled rooms while listening to the latest 'progressive rock' record.

But time went by, as it always does. All too suddenly I looked over my shoulder and found youth had passed. I'd left Wales when I was seventeen and had spent a few years in the army, then, astonishingly – as many who knew me as a soldier would probably have said – became a policeman. I began my career in Cheltenham – often called the 'Gateway to the Cotswolds' – and quickly learned about the rush of excitement that accompanies the arrest of a drunk or a shoplifter. Well, actually, it isn't much of a 'rush'. For me it was more of a trickle that was soon to run out completely. Still, I performed well enough, I believe, and it wasn't very long before I received a posting to the North Cotswolds town of Moreton-in-Marsh.

I took to the place immediately, and recognizing a good thing when I saw it, rapidly abandoned any idea of 'career advancement' and proceeded to put roots down. It was just as well, really. I subsequently went on to contract multiple sclerosis and found my strength and mobility somewhat diminished. I managed a good many more years as a policeman, however, before it was recommended that I take early retirement.

I went on to see the Cotswolds from a variety of angles, spending twelve years as a community constable in Moreton before moving to work, variously, at Stow-on-the-Wold, Bourton-on-the-Water and Cirencester – areas that colleagues from the urban centres of Cheltenham and Gloucester disparagingly called 'the blunt end'. The blunt end suited me nicely, though, and I was fortunate to encounter many interesting people and unusual situations during the course of my work. Over more than twenty years in the Cotswolds I came to know the district very well, not least because I had a number of hobbies and pursuits outside the police service. Back in Wales I had developed an early interest in history, archaeology and folklore, and this was something I continued in Gloucestershire. For many years, too, I had been attracted to anything that might be termed 'curious' – whether it be an ancient standing stone, a little-known beauty spot, a disused aerodrome, a folly erected by some eccentric egotist, or, perhaps, the site of an unsolved murder. In common with many parts of Britain, the Cotswolds has an abundance of such curiosities.

In 1993 my book *Folklore and Mysteries of the Cotswolds* was published and now I have produced this idiosyncratic work *Curious Cotswolds*. It is neither a definitive guide to the area (there are already plenty of those) nor an autobiography, though I suppose the reader will inevitably form an opinion about my character. Basically, it is aimed at the reader like me – someone who is drawn to the unusual – and it is my hope that it will be found readable, informative and … curious.

Many of the geographical features and ancient monuments described have changed comparatively little over the centuries, and it is likely they will remain relatively unchanged for many more years. Some features, though, will inevitably change – and in some cases disappear altogether – so it is recommended that, if interested, a visit is made sooner rather than later, particularly where the feature is not of great antiquity and may not enjoy special protection. My observations on village shops, pubs and the like merely provide a snapshot of the scene when I visited – in the main, during the early years of the twenty-first century – and cannot be taken as definitive.

Geographically, I have stuck fairly closely to the Cotswolds area within Gloucestershire, though it has been necessary to include sections on the neighbouring counties of Oxfordshire, Warwickshire and Worcestershire. Much of the information results from a combination of my own experiences and observation, and personal accounts volunteered by others. Obviously, though, numerous worthwhile books about the area have already been published, and where appropriate, I have acknowledged other writers and publications.

Various people have been of assistance to me during the writing of this book, but, in particular, I would like to acknowledge the help received from the following: Mary Boddington, Janina Bolan, Sean Bolan, Paul Bonner, Sylvia Charlewood, Beth Crabtree, Stephen Crabtree, Martin Dee, John Elliott, Bernie Green, Gerald Green, Jonathan Harley, Peter Harris, Brian Healey, Richard and Marilyn Hodkin, Tim Izod, Kerry Johnson, Oliver Lovell, David Minett, Margaret Moore, Jane Page, David Reynolds, John Scaife, Margaret Shepard, Guy Stapleton, Benjamin Turner and Samuel Turner.

Mark Turner
*February 2005*

# 1

# CHELTENHAM AND THE NORTH COTSWOLDS

Cheltenham is a particularly appropriate place for me to begin. Not only is it often called the 'Gateway to the Cotswolds', but it is the place where I began my time as a policeman. I had in fact received my first glimpse of Cheltenham several years earlier when the train on which I was travelling stopped briefly at the railway station. I was not impressed, and even today the station remains somewhat dreary in its appearance – though efforts have been made to brighten the place up. Fortunately it is not really representative of Cheltenham, which actually has much that is attractive and pleasing to the eye.

Cheltenham gained a reputation as an elegant spa town after King George III took the waters here in 1788. The town subsequently went from strength to strength, becoming known in the nineteenth century as a somewhat genteel retirement spot for army officers. Today it is probably best known as an upmarket shopping town and home of the Cheltenham Racecourse, where horses annually compete for the prestigious Gold Cup. During my stay in the town I lodged with an elderly lady in the St Marks area. Nearby was Coronation Square – an area that few would describe as the most salubrious in Cheltenham – and I recall occasionally calling for a drink at a pub named The Toby. It seemed to be much frequented by 'rough diamond' and 'salt of the earth' types but, to my recollection, was a friendly enough place. Today the pub's name has been changed to The Gold Cup, though I imagine 'rough diamonds' may still visit regularly.

Well away from Coronation Square there are some fine Regency buildings, a handsome promenade and pleasant parks, as well as some inviting shopping areas. My favourite park is Sandford Park, just off the Bath Road. It was opened in 1928, is fairly small and has the River Chelt (actually not much more than a fair-sized stream) running through it. The park offers shoppers a pleasant little haven off the main shopping area and I have taken advantage of this facility on many occasions. Just off the Promenade is the Regent Arcade, with some decent shops and, most

*The clock in Regent Arcade, Cheltenham.*

interestingly, a clock created in the 1980s by designer Kit Williams. Every hour, as chimes ring out and the tune 'I'm Forever Blowing Bubbles' is mechanically played, bubbles issue forth from the gaping mouth of a huge wooden fish suspended from the clock, accompanied by the devious antics of snakes and serpents. Actually, the Regent Arcade was constructed in the 1980s on the site of The Plough Hotel. I remember the old hotel very well – it was a regular bolt-hole for policemen on foot patrol of the town centre in the middle of the night. A kindly night porter would always make a cup of tea for the visiting officers who sometimes, it seemed, probably outnumbered the guests of the hotel.

To my mind, the nicest shopping area in the town is at Montpellier, just off the Promenade. Relaxed and perhaps a little Continental in style, Montpellier Street has pleasant dining establishments and a selection of shops that are individual and interesting. Not far away is Suffolk Parade, where the shops are equally interesting, and there is a superb wine bar named The Retreat. I have been visiting the establishment for more than twenty years and love the place. The food and wine are excellent, the décor is tasteful and modern, and the mainly female staff are all very nice looking. A great place to while away a couple of hours – who could ask for more?

A little way out of the centre, at No. 4 Clarence Road, is the Holst Birthplace Museum. In 1874 Gustav Holst, composer of The Planets suite, was born here, the son of a music teacher. After studying music his first professional engagement was as organist and choirmaster at Wyck Rissington church. He later went to the Royal College of Music and by 1903 had begun to concentrate on composing. He died in 1934. The house where he was born is today an interesting little museum.

Music of a very different sort was composed and played by Brian Jones, a founder member of perennial rock 'n' roll band The Rolling Stones. Jones was born in Cheltenham in 1942 and lived at No. 17 Eldorado Road (which bears a blue plaque commemorating this) until 1950, then subsequently moved to London, where he rented a flat with Mick Jagger and Keith Richard (no, not a spelling error – the 's' wasn't added to his surname until much later). The rest, as they say, is history. Unfortunately, Jones was a persistent drug-user, and in 1969, having become something of a liability to the band, left The Rolling Stones. Less than a month later, aged just twenty-seven, he was found dead in the swimming pool of his home at Hartfield, Sussex. The official cause of death was 'drowning while under the influence of alcohol and drugs', but rumours of murder – or, at the very least, manslaughter – have long persisted. Certainly Jones was a major talent in the rock world of his day, and his death was acutely felt in Cheltenham, where the streets were lined with people at his funeral. His grave is still visited by fans, and may be seen near the chapel in the cemetery off Bouncers Lane. Also of interest is a bronze bust of Jones that in 2005 was erected in Cheltenham's Beechwood Shopping Arcade. Fans of the 'old rockers' of the '60s are well catered for in Cheltenham. The Town Hall in Imperial Square often presents acts from that decade, as well as contemporary musicians representing an eclectic range of styles. I have enjoyed many an evening's entertainment there, but – be warned – the hall is known as something of an acoustic 'black hole', so it is wise to obtain seating towards the front.

One of the nicest areas of Cheltenham is Charlton Kings, originally a separate village but now more or less a suburb of the town. The Church of St Mary, with its fifteenth-century tower, has a Norman font, beautifully carved and reshaped in the fourteenth century. At the west end of the church is the particularly lovely Rose Window, which dates from 1823. In the Chantry, now St David's Chapel, is a fine old oak alms chest, fashioned from a solid log of wood. This is thought perhaps to date from 1190 – certainly it is very old indeed. On the other side of town the lower High Street runs past the former St Paul's Maternity Hospital and on to

*Brian Jones' grave, Cheltenham.*

Gloucester Road. A trip past the old hospital entrance evokes memories in me of how, as a policeman stationed in the town, I became friendly with a young midwife working in the maternity unit. She was a lovely girl, but I was subsequently moved to pastures new at Moreton-in-Marsh and was too immature to properly appreciate her, so we parted. Oh well, no sense in getting melancholy…

Setting aside thoughts of happy times at the nurses' home, we move on to The Hop Pole public house in Gloucester Road, where there is a plaque on the wall which indicates the site of an early horse tram road terminus. The Gloucester and Cheltenham Railway operated from 1809 until 1861, connecting the Gloucester and Berkeley Canal at Gloucester to Cheltenham, with a branch running to a quarry at Leckhampton – like Charlton Kings, technically a separate village, but now a suburb of Cheltenham. Leckhampton Quarry – today long-disused and a local beauty spot – is the location of Cheltenham's most famous landmark. The 'Devil's Chimney' is a curious pinnacle of rock detached from the Cotswold edge, formed by quarrymen who, apparently, left the rock in place because it was of an inferior standard to that which surrounded it, and therefore of no use for building purposes. It has long presented a challenge to local young climbers, and thirteen people once stood on its top. Climbing and erosion have, over the years, taken their toll and in recent times thousands of pounds have been spent on repairs.

Finally, a gruesome tale of murder and mystery has a Leckhampton connection. In January 1938 some bloodstained garments were found in the River Severn near Haw Bridge at Tirley, but interest soon faded as official doubt was expressed as to whether the blood was actually human. Then, a couple of weeks later, one Brian Sullivan was found dead in his home at Tower Lodge, Leckhampton, apparently having committed suicide. Soon after, there were more macabre finds at Haw Bridge in the form of a man's headless and limbless torso, weighted down in the river with bricks. Meanwhile a retired army officer named Captain William Butt had gone missing from his home at Cheltenham's Old Bath Road and a connection was established between Butt and Sullivan, a professional dancer. Police believed the headless trunk to be that of Butt, and a major search, including digging of the garden, commenced at Tower Lodge. Scotland Yard became involved, and Sir Bernard Spilsbury, the eminent pathologist, conducted the autopsy on the human remains. Butt's bloodstained coat was found concealed at Tower Lodge and Sullivan's mother – widely regarded as an accomplice – was interviewed by police, but no new evidence was forthcoming and at the subsequent inquest the jury returned a verdict of 'murder of a person or persons unknown'. There the mystery remains; a distant memory of an unsolved murder. Tower Lodge still stands at its position almost opposite Daisy Bank Road but has been much altered since the days when it was the scene of such excitement, and few nowadays recall its grisly history.

So much, then, for Cheltenham and its curious places. Attractive and popular though Cheltenham is, I prefer these days to enjoy the quieter life in the villages and small towns of the Cotswolds hills. Taking the A40 road east out of the town, and past the reservoir at Dowdeswell, one finds a road on the left to Whittington after about four miles. The village has some pretty cottages and a handsome manor house, the sixteenth-century Whittington Court. The church has three fourteenth-century effigies, but perhaps the most interesting curiosity in Whittington is its wayside well. This stone well is built into the low wall of the garden of No. 33 in the village. It is of a triangular structure with a recessed water spout, which leads into a rectangular stone trough. The whole structure is in a semi-ruinous condition – there is a hole in the back of the fountain, and the trough is crumbling. Inscribed in stone on the fountain wall above the spout are the words:

WASTE NOT WANT NOT

A small metal bath has been placed in the trough and a stone slab carved with the message: 'PLEASE HELP SAVE OUR FOUNTAIN' has been put in front of it. To my knowledge the bath has been there for at least a decade and one hopes funds for restoration are steadily accumulating. I tossed some coins into the bath, but I can't help thinking it will be a long wait if roadside collections are relied upon to provide the necessary funds.

Continuing for a short distance along the A40 towards Oxford, we arrive at the village of Andoversford. There are no outstanding features here. Just off the A436 road at Kilkenny, however, is a picnic area with a car park and information points. There are excellent views towards the Severn Valley and a pleasant drive may be taken along a minor road towards the A435 Cheltenham-Cirencester road near Colesbourne. This minor road passes St Paul's Epistle, a small tree-topped round barrow, and on through Pinchley Wood and Mercombe Wood.

My police duty performed at Andoversford was usually in the form of a presence at the twice-yearly horse sale held in fields above the village. One of my specialist roles was as 'Wildlife Liaison Officer', which involved working with the RSPCA to ensure any animals offered for sale were being properly treated. I was also in charge of running the 'Horsewatch' scheme – quite amusing when one considers that I have never ridden a horse in my life.

After a few miles the A40 reaches the small town of Northleach. About a mile north-west, however, is Hampnett, a quiet village with a large green. The church is mainly Norman and has some unusual stencil work on its interior walls, which, when seen for the first time, can be quite startling. In the 1870s the village rector, the Reverend Wiggins, began painting the interior of the church in a variety of patterns, reminiscent of the medieval period. The painting work, of flowers and angels, in colours of yellow, blue, green and terracotta, creates a surprisingly peaceful setting. It may be that the paintings followed earlier designs. Also of interest are finely carved birds on the capitals supporting the chancel arch, which provide a good example of Norman craftsmanship.

Nearby, the little town of Northleach is bypassed by the busy A40 – until the early 1980s the road ran through the centre of the town – and has a quiet and relaxed feel about it. The High Street is lined with pleasant shops, inns and houses dating from the sixteenth to the nineteenth century, but the town's splendid 'wool' church is the real gem, with its fine tower and pinnacled south porch. During the Middle Ages Northleach was second only to Chipping Campden and Cirencester as a centre for wool trading.

To the west of the town, at the side of the Fosse Way, is Northleach's former prison and original police station, built around 1789 by Sir Onesiphorous Paul – not much likelihood of *his* name being duplicated very often! The building has not been used as a 'house of correction' for a great many years, however. Today the building is home to 'The Cotswold Heritage Centre', an interesting museum

*The Church Interior, Hampnett.*

that gives access to the former prison and to an interesting collection of rural artefacts.

Heading east into the town centre, one finds a residence named Walton House situated opposite the Market Place. During the Second World War, twelve pilots from 87 Fighter Squadron stayed there while they flew from Bibury airfield during the Battle of Britain in 1940. In 2004 a plaque to commemorate the billeting of the pilots was unveiled at the house. A little further along the road is Oak House, home to 'Keith Harding's World of Mechanical Music'. More than a museum, this is a marvellous collection of all sorts of mechanical instruments, musical boxes and wind-up music machines. There are regular demonstrations of these intriguing things 'at work'.

Just over a mile to the north-east of Northleach, situated on a lane that runs close to the Sherborne Brook, and subsequently the lovely River Windrush, stands the tiny village of Farmington. It has a Norman church and an extensive village green, upon which stands an attractive octagonal well, with eight gables, a stone roof and

*The Ornate Bus Shelter at Farmington.*

a small cupola. Dated 1898, and 50-60ft deep, it originally supplied all the nearby houses. The green and well make a particularly endearing and peaceful Cotswold scene, especially when one considers that the busy A40 and A429 roads are actually quite near.

The village bus shelter is a remarkably attractive little stone building. Of hexagonal shape, with a stone tiled roof topped by a finial, it stands opposite the junction of the two lanes that lead to Northleach and the A429 respectively. Designed by Northleach resident Gerald Green, it was constructed by the people of Farmington, using local materials, and won a prize in a competition held during the Festival of Britain in 1951. Sadly, it looks to be little used nowadays, and undergrowth is beginning to encroach upon it.

The lane running north-east from the village to Bourton-on-the-Water is very pleasant and offers an opportunity to approach Bourton from an especially pretty angle. Heading east towards Burford, however, one soon arrives at the delightful village of Sherborne – much of which is owned by the National Trust – situated in the valley of the Sherborne Brook, which has for part of its length been widened, the alteration creating a picturesque weir. In the sixteenth century the estate of

Sherborne was owned by 'Crump' Dutton, the hunchback Royalist who 'backed both sides' in the Civil War. He had Valentine Strong, quarry owner and builder of great note, from nearby Taynton, enhance Sherborne Park (rebuilt in the nineteenth century), which is today a development of luxury flats. Sherborne's church of St Mary Magdelene stands next to the house, and though much rebuilt in the nineteenth century, has a medieval tower and spire. In the interior there is a fine monument by Richard Westmacott the Elder, signed and dated 1791, to James Lenox Dutton. It depicts an angel trampling upon a hideous figure of death, and is almost ghoulish in its representation. Also inside the church is a brass memorial plaque to James Bradley, one of Britain's greatest astronomers, who was born in Sherborne in 1693, attending school at nearby Northleach. In 1742 he was appointed Astronomer Royal.

Valentine Strong is thought also to have built the lovely seventeenth-century dower-house, Lodge Park, near Sherborne. I remember how, in the early 1980s, I was called upon to stay up all night inside the house with a detective colleague. Information had apparently been received suggesting a burglary would take place, and we were the lucky ones who were meant to apprehend the thieves. In the event, the burglary didn't happen, so all my shadow boxing was in vain!

Just behind Lodge Park is a long barrow, as yet unexcavated. It measures 150ft long by 70ft wide and at the south-east end two uprights and a lintel stone show through the grass. In her book *A Guide to the Prehistoric and Roman Monuments in England and Wales*, Jacquetta Hawkes describes the barrow as 'quite exceptionally unspoiled', and in his *Long Barrows of the Cotswolds* O.G.S. Crawford says 'This is the finest long barrow I have ever seen'.

At the east end of the village is a nineteenth-century cottage - No. 88 - which has two twelfth-century doorways. The doorway facing the road has a carved tympanum and chevron and zigzag ornament. These are thought to be the remains of the village's original Norman church, believed to have stood in a field almost opposite.

The lane past the cottage leads on to the village of Windrush, a little over a mile towards Burford. A tranquil and attractive place, Windrush has a triangular green overlooked by some attractive houses and a handsome church, notable especially for its fine Norman south doorway. The church has much of interest, including a Jacobean pulpit, a medieval screen, a fifteenth-century font and some medieval floor tiles. In the churchyard there are several eighteenth-century table tombs, and of special interest to the curiosity-seeker is a stone plaque that has been set into the wall around the churchyard. This is inscribed to the memory of Sgt Bruce Hancock RAFVR, who 'sacrificed his life by ramming and destroying an enemy Heinkel bomber' in 1940.

*A detail of Richard Westmacott's monument to James Lenox Dutton in Sherborne Church: 'the hideous figure of death'.*

*The Long Barrow at Lodge Park.*

*One of the twelfth-century doorways from the cottage at the east end of Sherborne.*

On 18 August of that year, Hancock was flying an unarmed Anson training aircraft from RAF Little Rissington airfield when he encountered a German Heinkel bomber, which had just dropped several high explosive bombs in the area. The bomber, which was probably returning from a raid on Coventry, began peppering the Anson with machine gun fire. According to witnesses, Hancock then doused the lights of his plane, banked to port, then pulled up suddenly and rammed into the Heinkel.

It is possible that this was the erratic action of a crippled aircraft, but it is known that Hancock had previously said that if faced with attack while flying an unarmed aircraft he would try to ram his attacker.

As a result of Hancock's action, the Heinkel crashed in flames close to Blackpits Barn, near Aldsworth village. The German crew of five were killed and buried in the churchyard at Northleach. In the 1950s relatives of these airmen occasionally visited the graves, but in about 1965 the coffins were lifted and placed in a cemetery holding other German war dead. The plaque on the wall of Windrush churchyard was installed in the 1980s, when around 150 people – including wartime pilots, senior RAF officers, and personnel who had served at Windrush airfield in the Second World War – attended a ceremony, at which there was an RAF fly-past.

Less than a mile east, and just three miles from Burford (in Oxfordshire), is Little Barrington. The village is dominated by a large green, which was once a quarry. The grass is a little rough, and the green is rather less manicured-looking than those of many Cotswold villages. This gives the village, with its houses crowded around the slopes of the green, less of a 'chocolate-box' appearance than some villages in the area – and it is all the more pleasing for that.

For centuries Barrington stone was quarried at the village and was used all over the country – notably at St Paul's Cathedral, Blenheim Palace, St George's Chapel, Windsor and many of the colleges at Oxford. By the nineteenth century the stone was being mined underground, though the mines were closed by the early twentieth century. Quarries still in use at that time had been closed by 1961.

Stone was taken by barge to London from the Windrush to the Thames, and on to Paul's Wharf. On the north side of Little Barrington a spot near The Fox Inn is known locally as 'the Wharf' and a few hundred yards lower down on the Windrush there are faint remains of a sloping weir of stone where the water level could be raised to allow the stone-laden barges to float over, in order to avoid the mill race below. Nearby is an attractive three-arch stone bridge, built about 1740. This, however, is on private property. The Windrush at this point has been diverted and widened to form a stretch of ornamental water.

The Fox Inn is worth a visit. It is in a lovely setting on the banks of the Windrush, and serves fine ales from Donnington Brewery. From the inn, if one crosses the bridge over the Windrush and takes the lane up the hill towards Great Barrington, it is possible to catch a glimpse of one of the follies of Barrington Park. It is a small temple and is situated high up on the bank to the left of the road.

Unusually quaint in its rural setting on the edge of the village is Little Barrington's Reading Room. This gives a lovely view across the Windrush towards Great Barrington. I recall how, as a Crime Prevention Officer, I held a 'crime prevention display' in this charming building on a lovely summer's day in the 1990s. I don't suppose more than a dozen people actually visited it, but those that did come were enthusiastic, and my appreciation of the Reading Room and its enchanting view over the Cotswold fields of Oxfordshire and Gloucestershire was considerable.

Across the River Windrush is Great Barrington. This small village in the Windrush Valley has a number of charming cottages and houses. Many had become unoccupied and had fallen into disrepair through the mid-to-late twentieth century, but restoration is well under way, so the community's former 'ghost village' appearance is fading. Prominent in Great Barrington is the Palladian mansion of Barrington Park (erected in 1736-8 for Earl Talbot), though the lovely house and much of the park in which it is situated is hidden from view by a tall stone wall. The limited view through fine eighteenth-century wrought-iron gates, with stone piers and ball-finials, on the road towards Great Rissington does, however, reveal one of the eighteenth-century follies that stands in the park. Another view can be had from the roadside across to the parkland – but not of the house or follies – where there is a ha-ha. A ha-ha is a sunken fence or ditch and it is placed to keep the deer in the park without the need for unsightly walls or fences.

The Church of St Mary the Virgin at Great Barrington is largely Norman, but the chancel was entirely rebuilt in 1880. The nave, however, has a thirteenth-century north arcade and is of more interest. One monument, in particular, is rather touching. Carved of marble, an angel leads two children by the hand to walk on the clouds. Edward Bray, aged fifteen, and his sister, Jane, aged eight, died of smallpox in 1720 and 1711 respectively. The monument was designed by Francis Bird and carved by Christopher Cass.

The next stop on this 'tour' involves taking the lane north out of Great Barrington until, after about two miles, one arrives at Great Rissington. This is a pleasant village looking over the Windrush valley. The church has a fifteenth-century tower and in its porch there is a fifteenth-century carving of the Crucifixion. In his 1938 book *The King's England: Gloucestershire*, Arthur Mee mentions the church peace memorial, on which the five sons of a Mrs W. Souls are recorded as having been lost in the First World War. The loss of young men in that dreadful conflict was indeed very heavy, but to lose five sons must have been exceptional. As Arthur Mee says: '…perhaps the costliest sacrifice made by any English mother … she was only a poor woman and was happy with her boys, and five times the terrible news came to her in the war that she had lost a son…' After the war, Mrs Souls went to live in Great Barrington, where she died in 1935.

Below Great Rissington's small triangular green is a welcoming hostelry The Lamb Inn, a popular place for eating and drinking. Displayed on the wall above the fireplace inside the lounge bar is a memorial plaque to five airmen who died in a plane crash close to the inn during the Second World War. Also displayed is part of a propeller and other relics from the crash, together with photographs of the crew. In the early hours of 8 October 1943 a Wellington bomber from the aerodrome at Moreton-in-Marsh attempted to make an emergency landing at RAF Little Rissington, after the port engine failed. The station diary for RAF Moreton-in-Marsh records that:

> The pilot positioned himself and made a right-hand approach. On the turn in he found difficulty in controlling the aircraft, throttled back, lost height, and hit the ground…

Of the crew of six, all were killed except the rear gunner, Sgt Smith, who was seriously injured. It was ex-Sgt Smith who, in 1988, arranged for the placing of the poignant memorial to his comrades.

From the unclassified road towards Bourton-on-the-Water there is a tree-lined lane, marked 'unsuitable for motors', leading to Clapton-on-the-Hill. This lane leads to the River Windrush, crossing via New Bridge, before climbing the hill to Clapton. New Bridge is a truly delightful place, quiet and unspoilt, the sight of which is worth the drive along a somewhat unserviceable roadway.

Clapton-on-the-Hill is a small village with excellent views eastwards across the Windrush valley from a little green on a steep slope in the centre. The green, with a bench from which the view can be enjoyed, is a particularly pleasant feature in what is, essentially, a rural working village with cottages, some eighteenth-century barns and fine farmhouses with mullioned windows. There is a very small thirteenth-century church, supposed to be the smallest in Gloucestershire, the nave measuring just 30ft by 13ft. Entry to the churchyard is through an interesting churchyard gate made from horseshoes.

Bourton-on-the-Water is a short drive north from Clapton-on-the-Hill. Bourton is not my favourite village in the Cotswolds. Some call it 'The Venice of The Cotswolds'; I call it 'The Blackpool of The Cotswolds'. Unfortunately, though stationed in the village for a short time in the 1990s, I cannot say the place holds particularly fond memories for me. My time seemed to consist mainly of dealing with domestic disputes at an edge-of-village housing estate or trying to pacify violent drunks intent on committing damage or assault in one or two of the village centre pubs. Also, of course, the summer season's influx of tourists always brought seemingly endless traffic jams and parking problems.

But perhaps my summary is a little unfair. Bourton is actually a very pretty village and there is much to commend it. Its ornamental bridges over the River Windrush are famous and its many attractions cater for the huge number of tourists who visit throughout the summer season. The discerning visitor will probably best appreciate Bourton when it is somewhat quieter, though, and for this reason I suggest visiting in the spring or autumn. Before dealing with the village's curiosities, I will briefly describe what I believe to be the best tourist attractions.

In the High Street is the Model Railway exhibition. This comprises three large layouts that, for children and lovers of model railways, will prove fascinating. To the uninitiated, of course, one model railway looks much like any other, so this exhibition will have limited appeal. Even so, it is worth a visit.

Housed in a pretty water mill across the road from the Model Railway is the Cotswold Motor Museum. As well as the inevitable veteran cars, there are scores of interesting bits and pieces from bygone ages, including a good collection of enamel advertising signs. Of great appeal to children is the original miniature car named 'Brum', as featured on the popular children's television series. I think this is a super little museum.

In nearby Victoria Street is the Perfumery Exhibition, where there is a presentation on the history of perfume and the opportunity to visit the perfume garden, where all the plants have been chosen for their fragrance. There is a laboratory, too, where visitors may test the products.

Back to the High Street, then, and on to Rissington Road. Here one finds The Old New Inn, one of the best hostelries in the village. Behind the inn is Bourton's famous Model Village, which was created in the 1930s by the inn's owner, who had decided to make his vegetable garden into something more decorative. Every house in Bourton was measured and each building was built to one-ninth scale, local people helping to complete the project. Opened in 1937 on the Coronation Day of King George VI, it has over the years attracted many thousands of visitors.

Carrying on along Rissington Road, one arrives at two attractions situated close together. The first of these is the Dragonfly Maze – a yew hedge maze, with over a quarter of a mile of pathways. Opened in 1997, it was designed by artist and writer Kit Williams, and has engraved flagstones along its pathways, providing clues that lead one to an ornate central pavilion. This houses the bronze 'Minotoad', enabling one to discover the 'Golden Dragonfly'. The perambulation around the deceptively complex maze is fun for all ages, this relatively recent addition to Bourton's tourist attractions proving very popular.

Almost next door is the village's very well known 'Birdland', a large and attractive home to a variety of bird species. It first opened in 1957 in the centre of the village, moving to its present position in 1989. The sanctuary includes a penguin display, always very popular at feeding time. I remember being on police duty when, in the 1980s, Anneka Rice visited Bourton for the *Treasure Hunt* TV programme. I had to smile at the finished programme, in which I could be seen beaming happily as Anneka sprinted by. I wonder if any viewers guessed that my convivial smile was actually in appreciation of the lady's shapely bottom!

As well as the tourist attractions, there are several other places worth visiting. A little further along Rissington Road the cricket ground will be seen on the left. Next to this is a path leading to Cemetery Lane. This is the best approach to the village's 'Quarry Lakes', flooded gravel pits on which nature reserves are now established. Pleasant walks can be taken in the vicinity of these lakes.

Returning to the village itself, there is a functional business park off Station Road. At the side of the road leading into the business park is Bourton's Railway

Station – sadly, not used as such for more than forty years. From 1862 to 1962 a railway ran from Banbury to Cheltenham, a branch line from Kingham terminating at Bourton-on-the-Water. As can be seen, the station was conveniently situated, less than half a mile from the centre of the village, but now all trace of the line running past the station has long since been removed and the building is used to store road signs. This station building dates from the early 1930s and replaced an earlier half-timbered building. In 2003 the Gloucestershire Warwickshire Railway, which operates steam trains from Toddington Railway Station, announced plans to dismantle the station stone by stone and re-erect it at Broadway. Some years earlier the preservation society had carried out a similar operation by dismantling Troy Station at Monmouth and re-erecting it near Winchcombe. I hope this plan comes to fruition – it would be nice to see the building properly used once more.

The parish church, as the only church in the Cotswolds to have an eighteenth-century classical tower, should not be missed. Crowned by a somewhat incongruous-looking lead dome, it was built around 1784, by a local man called William Marshall. The south porch, with its ogee arch and big cusps, was the subject of a Royal Academy drawing in 1890. The chancel is medieval and has a new roof, beautifully painted in 1928 by F.E. Howard. There are several excellently carved table-tombs and headstones in the churchyard, particularly one to a man named Jordan.

I've only once attended a service at this church, and sadly, that was for the funeral of an ex-colleague. At the Baptist church in Station Road, however, I have been present at several memorable musical gatherings, when various musicians from the rock world – Mike Kelly, Jess Roden, Ruby Turner and Steve Winwood, to name just a few – have performed. These superb concerts became an almost annual event through the 1990s, though I often wondered if the local residents were aware of the wealth of talent playing in a little church up the road.

Also worth visiting is Bourton Bridge, which crosses the River Windrush near the A429 junction with the A436 road to Cheltenham. Best seen from the footpath running alongside the river, this pretty bridge is on the site of a Roman bridge. In the eighth century there was a ford here, and a stone bridge in 1483, though this was completely rebuilt in 1806. In 1959 further rebuilding and widening took place to create the bridge that exists today. From this point a pleasant walk can be taken across fields to the village of Naunton, where sustenance may be obtained at The Black Horse public house.

On the north-west of Bourton is the A429 (Fosse Way). If one follows this road for a short distance towards Stow-on-the-Wold, a lane on the right leads to Wyck Rissington. This unspoilt village has a long green with charming cottages along much of its length. On the green is a drinking fountain and there is a pretty duck

*The bus shelter at Wyck Rissington.*

pond nearby. Near the pond is an unusually attractive bus shelter, put up for the Queen's Coronation in 1953.

Until about 1980 a fascinating maze of 'the Mysteries of the Gospel' could be seen in the garden of the old rectory, near the church of St Lawrence – created by Canon Harry Cheales, the rector for more than thirty years. He constructed the maze in 1950, following a vivid dream, but after his retirement in 1980 the rectory was sold off and the maze cleared away. On the north wall of the church nave there is a mosaic reproduction of the maze, made of Italian marble from the same quarry used by Michelangelo.

The church has a thirteenth-century tower and chancel, and there is stone benching along the south wall and part of the north wall. The south stained glass window is particularly interesting. It depicts the Crucifixion, with the sun, moon and two stars behind the figure. There is a theory that the sun illustrates the eclipse of 1322.

The lane through Wyck Rissington soon leads to Little Rissington, where there is a former wartime aerodrome. The village overlooks the flooded gravel pits of nearby Bourton-on-the-Water, but there is not a great deal else to see. The Church of St Peter is reached by a path across a field. It has two arches dating from the twelfth century and the chancel is thirteenth century, with additions having taken place over the next couple of centuries. There is a fifteenth-century font and outside in the churchyard there are numerous graves and monuments to men who died in the Second World War while stationed at the nearby airfield. Little Rissington was for many years home to the Central Flying School, from where the Red Arrows aerobatic team flew, and a number of the pilots were regular visitors to local hostelries like The Fox Inn at Little Barrington. When the Central Flying School left Rissington in 1976, the base was taken on by the army, becoming Imjin Barracks. By the early 1980s, however, the army had gone and the barracks were deserted. On patrol around the former aerodrome in the early 1980s I recall thinking what a waste of perfectly good accommodation it was. It felt quite eerie patrolling around deserted streets and houses, especially when it was considered that just a few years earlier they would have been busy with troops and families. The USAF subsequently took over in 1982 and I remember using the guardroom as a handy place to stop off for a coffee when on night patrol. The Americans have now gone and many of the old military houses have been taken into civilian ownership, and the former RAF Little Rissington has become a new community and parish named Upper Rissington.

The small village of Westcote lies a little over a mile to the east. It is divided into two halves – Church Westcote and Nether Westcote – and is to be found down a lane that leads off the A424 road. Fine views over the Evenlode Valley can be had from a lane running between the two, and there is a stone pedestal and topograph that illustrates the various points of interest. At Nether Westcote there is a welcoming hostelry, The New Inn.

Returning to the A424, it is just over two miles to Stow-on-the-Wold. Approaching the A429, down the hill on the A424, one sees an imposing mansion high on a hill ahead. This is Quarwood, and was home of John Entwistle, legendary bass guitarist with rock band The Who until his untimely death in 2002. Some years ago I had been writing about Keith Moon, the band's deceased drummer, and on the off-chance that John would speak to me, called at Quarwood. Not only did John read through the work I had done, but he wrote a foreword for another project I was completing, showed me around his studio, invited me to share a bottle of wine with him in his 'Barracuda Inn' and got me tickets sitting next to his mum, Queenie, at a forthcoming concert by The Who at London's Earls Court. Definitely one of the 'gentlemen of rock'!

Stow-on-the-Wold is noted for its market square, surrounded by shops and hotels, and its twice-yearly horse fair. The sale of horses has now been moved to Andoversford, but stalls selling 'country fayre', puppies and other animals, junk and miscellanea are to be seen in May and October, crowding the verges along the lane from Stow to Maugersbury. The Square has a number of lovely seventeenth-

and eighteenth-century stone buildings and the church is worth a visit for the Crucifixion painting in the south aisle.

Stow has numerous hotels and inns, most of a very good standard, but some of course are more interesting than others. On the front of The Talbot Hotel building there is a brass box in which, years ago, farmers would leave packets of grain for the corn merchants to test for quality. Also, at the front of The Old Stocks Hotel, and invariably covered by a large flower tub, a tombstone memorial is set into the paving at the front of the building. Apparently this is a remnant from a gravestone that once existed at the back of the hotel building.

A peculiar building can be seen at Sheep Street, which forms part of the A436 leading from Stow-on-the-Wold to Chipping Norton. A castellated folly was built here in 1848 by a man named Mr Enoch. Four storeys high, it apparently housed an unofficial museum at one time.

Unfortunately, though Enoch's name lives on in Stow as that of a noted eccentric, little seems to be known about him or his museum collection. He died in 1858 and is buried in Stow's cemetery.

The stone fountain that stands on the roadside at the junction of the High Street and Fosse Way was originally sited on the other side of the road, close to the junction of the Fosse Way and the Evesham Road. Its present position is the former site of a horse pool, filled-in in 1895. The fountain was presented to the town in 1896 by one Piers Thursby, but was badly damaged in a road accident (when it still stood close to the opposite junction) in 1963. It was rebuilt in 1966 where it now stands. For some years it had a somewhat neglected and untidy appearance, but in 2003 was substantially improved, with a neat paved area being laid around it.

Until 1868 the drinking water for the people of Stow-on-the-Wold came from a well situated 100 yards or so down the track from Stow to Broadwell. This well – known as the Upper Well – comes from a spring that flows into a rectangular stone trough, about 15ft long. A second well, a short distance down the hill towards Broadwell, is much smaller. The precise age of the Upper Well is not known, though it dates from at least the sixteenth century. Water was obtained, too, from St Edward's Well at the foot of Stow Hill and by cart from Lower Swell, though this situation was far from satisfactory, neither well providing enough water for the requirements of Stow's residents.

In the early nineteenth century attempts were made to turn Stow into a prosperous spa town to rival the likes of Cheltenham and Bath. A well rich in mineral deposits was discovered at nearby Lower Swell and was housed in a building known as Spa Cottage. A romantic pleasure garden known as The Retreat was created to the east of the fosse way, near the top of the hill at Stow-on-the-Wold. There was

Above: *Upper Well at Stow-on-the-Wold*.

Left: *St Edward's Well at Stow-on-the-Wold*.

a wooded walk, with a path leading through a tunnel beneath Maugersbury Lane, and on down to the foot of the hill, where refreshments could be obtained at a cottage. Though the trees and undergrowth are today almost impenetrable in parts, this area was laid out with paths and was much visited by the people of Stow-on-the-Wold when this was a continuation of The Retreat. Artificial pools and a stream could be visited in the woodland and St Edward's Well nearby was reputed to have healing properties especially beneficial to the eyes. Close to the well stood a gazebo. The well is still there, with the ruins of the stone gazebo close by. The identity of St Edward is uncertain, but he is thought to be St Edward the Saxon King, St Edward the Confessor, or a local hermit called Edward. The pleasure garden was, together with the Spa Cottage at Lower Swell, part of the attempt to popularise Stow as a resort.

Half a mile south-east of Stow-on-the-Wold is the very pretty hamlet of Maugersbury, which has an interesting history. In about 1800 the Lord of the Manor, Edmund John Chamberlayne, set about making the place into a 'model village'. Many of the cottages and smaller houses were rebuilt, and a striking building known as The Crescent was constructed. A semi-circular building with an internal diameter of 48ft, it was created as a row of four workers' cottages, the building originally including a Sunday school room, a communal bread oven, and a furnace and coal store. It is said that every family in The Crescent was given an acre of land and a pig, the gift of Edmund Chamberlayne. Today the building is called Half Moon House. Panoramic views are to be had from the lane that leads to the fosse way, this walk leading to Stow's former pleasure garden, The Retreat, and Maugersbury Arch, the tunnel that once allowed one to walk under the lane. The trees on Stow Hill, and on the former Retreat garden, are tall and impressive. Quite a few were brought down in the hurricane of 1987, but enough remain to ensure the place still has the feel of a 'secret garden'.

Next, the village of Oddington is found if one takes the A436 road east out of Stow, towards Chipping Norton. The village of Oddington is in two halves – 'Upper' and 'Lower' – and though the whole place is appealing and has two excellent pubs (The Horse and Groom at 'Upper' and The Fox at 'Lower') it is Lower Oddington that possesses the real gem.

The delightful Church of St Nicholas dates from the twelfth century, though a new nave and chancel were built in the thirteenth century, with further building in the fifteenth century. Deep grooves in the stone seats of the fourteenth-century porch indicate that arrows were sharpened there for many years. The building has a fine, tall Jacobean pulpit, and a good flagstone floor. Most notable, however, is the marvellous 'doom' painting on the nave wall. It dates from about 1480, but in the

*Maugersbury Arch.*

seventeenth century the interior of the building was whitewashed. The painting was thus concealed until 1912, when it was rediscovered and work begun to restore it. The church had been more or less deserted when in 1852 a second church was built in the village, and it was becoming dilapidated until 1912, when a new rector was appointed and began work to rescue the old church building. The church, standing alone down a narrow lane that leads along a bridle path to Bledington, is very much worth seeing.

From Oddington it is but a stone's throw to Adlestrop. I particularly like this small and quiet village in the valley of the River Evenlode, which has among its charms several pretty eighteenth-century cottages and a couple of lakes. It has a nicely kept churchyard, too, though the church itself is described by most guides as 'disappointing' and 'over-restored'. Jane Austen used to visit her uncle at the rectory here and Adlestrop Park has an ornate south-west front designed by Sanderson Miller, but the village is perhaps best known as the subject of Edward Thomas's evocative poem *Adlestrop*. Written in 1915, it recalls his brief visit by steam train to the station:

> Yes. I remember Adlestrop…
> The name, because one afternoon
> Of heat the express-train drew up there
> Unwontedly. It was late June.

The steam hissed. Someone cleared his throat.
No one left and no one came
On the bare platform. What I saw
Was Adlestrop…only the name.

And willows, willow-herb, and grass,
And meadowsweet, and haycocks dry,
No whit less still and lonely fair
Than the high cloudlets in the sky.

And for that minute a blackbird sang
Close by, and around him, mistier,
Farther and farther, all the birds
Of Oxfordshire and Gloucestershire.

Thomas died on active service in 1917, and Adlestrop's railway station closed in 1966. The grass and willow-herb can still be seen near the crumbling remains of the station platforms, but nowadays the express trains hurry by on their way to Oxford or Worcester. The station sign and one of the station benches – bearing a small plaque that details the poem – can be seen, however, in a little roadside shelter on the edge of the village. Painted in Great Western Railway colours, these form an interesting and unusual tribute to Edward Thomas.

The lane through Adlestrop soon leads to the pretty village of Evenlode, with its lovely old farmhouses and broad green. There is always a good fête on the green in the summer, with a coconut shy, cake stalls and other attractions. I remember it being opened one year in the 1980s by the actor Derek Nimmo, who gave a very witty and amusing address. Until 1969, the village had its own pub, The Fox, overlooking the green. In the 1980s, when I often cycled to Evenlode – sometimes on police duty, sometimes purely for a pleasant ride – I would call at the former pub, where I knew the former licensees, and enjoy a glass or two of whisky.

The lane from Evenlode to Moreton-in-Marsh is particularly pleasant, and each year in May there is a lovely display of bluebells forming a dense carpet on either side of the road in the woods of Evenlode Mane – next to the junction with the lane to the Chipping Norton road. I can remember how, back in 1990, I was standing on the roadside near these woods when I saw the wing of a plane tumble from the sky and land on the ground a few fields away. Tragically, a mid-air collision between a motorised glider and a light aircraft had occurred, and though

*The station sign at Adlestrop.*

the plane safely managed an emergency landing, the glider's two occupants were killed. Fifteen years later, in December 2005, a second mid-air collision took place between two planes flying in the locality. Though one managed to land safely near Lower Lemington, the other plunged to the ground at the Fire Service College, Moreton-in-Marsh, killing the pilot.

Evenlode's Norman church on the edge of the village has a fine chancel arch and a splendid carved fifteenth-century pulpit. In the churchyard there are a number of interesting eighteenth- and nineteenth-century tombs. On the southern edge of the village there is an interesting little cottage where one can buy pottery made on the premises, and from Horn Lane, on the eastern edge, there is the start of a very pleasant walk across the fields to nearby Chastleton. The lovely River Evenlode flows past the western side of the village and it makes a timeless and pastoral scene when viewed from Stock Bridge, just beyond Evenlode, on the lane to Broadwell.

Broadwell, about a mile to the west of Evenlode, is very picturesque and has several fine seventeenth-century farmhouses, a shallow ford and a large green overlooked by a very hospitable inn. If you enjoy real ale and good food in a pleasant, rural atmosphere, The Fox Inn should do very nicely. First, though, make time to visit the Church of St Paul, just off the lane towards Stow. Parts of the building date from the twelfth century. The tympanum, carved with a Maltese Cross from a Norman doorway, has been rebuilt into the base of the tower, and in the porch are

Above: *A table-tomb in the churchyard at Broadwell.*

Right: *The battlefield indicator stone at Donnington.*

some carved stones, one of which is believed to be Saxon. In the churchyard, and of particular note, are several early seventeenth-century table-tombs with 'bale tops'. One has eight mourning figures – often called the 'weepers' – kneeling round it. Near the church is a giant yew tree, hundreds of years old, its trunk more than 20ft in circumference.

The excellent ales served at The Fox Inn are actually brewed at Donnington Brewery, just a couple of miles west of Broadwell. There is not a great deal to see at the actual hamlet of Donnington. There are several pretty cottages, there is a good view across the Evenlode Valley to the east, and the place is of historical significance in that it was here on 21 March 1646 that the Royalist troops under Lord Astley finally surrendered to the Parliamentarians at the end of the Civil War. A stone, about 5ft high, commemorating the battle, can be seen a short walk across a few fields towards Longborough.

To the west of the village, however, is the aforementioned brewery, thought to be one of the smallest traditional breweries in the country. Certainly it must be one of the most attractive. The brewery is in a former mill situated in a pretty cluster of stone buildings at the side of a beautiful lake, from which the River Dikler rises. The various buildings date from the eighteenth to the nineteenth centuries and are of local stone with Welsh slate roofs. In 1827 the mill was bought by Thomas Arkell, his descendant's Donnington Ales being established by 1865. This small brewery, which owns fifteen pubs in the area, has been owned and run by the Arkell family ever since and today is managed by the grandson of the founder. The brewery is not open to the public, but a panoramic view of the mill and its lovely setting can be seen from the small road which runs from Condicote to Donnington village. There are several Donnington Ales, the most commonly found being BB and SBA (a little stronger and sweeter than BB).

Back in the 1980s, while on police patrol in the area, I found myself at the brewery – quite by chance, you understand. I remember that Mr Arkell kindly showed me around, and the visit was concluded by my sampling a glass of ale. Television viewers were able to see the brewery in the mid-1980s, too, as it was featured on the popular *Treasure Hunt* programme.

If one heads north from Donnington along the A429, the next place to be reached is the town of Moreton-in-Marsh. I came to live in the town in 1981, and I think it no exaggeration to say it was the best move I ever made. I thoroughly enjoyed my time as a policeman in the town, the sight of me plodding around the streets soon becoming familiar to the residents. I quickly worked out where the best 'tea stops' were, and made almost daily visits to the railway signal box and hospital, where I always received a warm welcome. There are a number of inns and

*The Four Shire Stone, c. 1910.*

pubs in the town, too, to which I am certainly no stranger. All are welcoming and hospitable, though my personal favourite – my 'local' – is The Inn on the Marsh, in Stow Road. This pub (called The White Horse until 1992) has a light and airy conservatory restaurant area, and is very friendly and popular. And the landlord keeps a very good pint.

Moreton has a number of curiosities worth seeking out, too. The first of these can be seen about a mile to the east of the town, at the junction of the A44 road to Chipping Norton and the unclassified road to Great Wolford. An impressive limestone pedestal called the Four Shire Stone stands at the roadside. It originally marked the point at which the four counties of Gloucestershire, Oxfordshire, Warwickshire and Worcestershire met, though since 1931 Worcestershire has been absent, the 'island' of Evenlode being taken into Gloucestershire. Just over 4ft wide, and a good 15ft tall, the basic form of the stone is that of a classic pedestal topped with a sundial, ball and finial.

Mention of a stone at this location was first made in about 1540 by John Leland, Antiquary Royal to King Henry VIII, but this was not the present structure and may well have been a Roman milestone. The stone we see today is believed to date from the late sixteenth century. It is said that in the eighteenth and nineteenth centuries prize-fighting bouts would periodically be held there. Over the years the Four Shire Stone has suffered from traffic accident damage and the scrawling

*The commemorative stone at the former aerodrome in Moreton-in-Marsh.*

of graffiti, but today survives as an impressive waymark. I remember attending a number of traffic accidents at the location, and it was not unusual for policemen of the Thames Valley and Warwickshire forces to attend, too. Sometimes it virtually came to tossing a coin to see which officer would deal with the accident, though eventually I became able to precisely pinpoint the county boundary.

Heading back into Moreton along the A44, one passes the Fire Service College, which occupies the former site of a Second World War RAF station. Just outside the college perimeter, near the main entrance, a memorial stone has been erected to commemorate RAF Moreton-in-Marsh. In January 1941 the RAF arrived on the newly constructed aerodrome to begin the training of Wellington bomber crews. The aerodrome was allocated the name of 21 OTU (Operational Training Unit) and operated throughout the Second World War. There were many flying accidents, as the nearby War Cemetery bears testimony, but German aircraft attacked the aerodrome on only two occasions – in April 1941 two high explosive bombs fell on the landing ground, then a month later a few incendiaries fell on one of the dispersal points. There were no casualties from either attack. It continued as an RAF training establishment, until in 1955 the Fire Service began training service personnel there, the camp subsequently becoming an annexe to the Fire Service College at Dorking. In 1966 it was announced that the Fire Service Technical College was opening on the site, and when in 1981 the College at Dorking closed, the Moreton-in-Marsh establishment became the Fire Service College. A memorial stone to commemorate the Wellington bomber crews who lost their lives during the Second World War was erected by Fire Service officers based at the College in 1993. The runways remain in good order, as part of the fire service training ground, but these are not open to the public. Reasonable views of the old aerodrome can be had, however, from the road between Moreton-in-Marsh and Todenham.

A few other remnants of the aerodrome still remain: just off the road to Todenham a number of the dispersal points still exist and, almost hidden by roadside undergrowth, at the junction of the lanes to Todenham and Lower Lemington is an old pillbox, and in fields to the east of the College perimeter there is a derelict brick building, originally a small arms ammunition store. For quite some years during the 1980s and '90s I remember a chap named John residing in the old store. It must have been a cold and lonely existence. Certainly he would engage me in lengthy conversation whenever I drove the police car to that rather isolated spot.

Moreton's War Cemetery is contained within the town's main cemetery, on the eastern fringe of the town, near the Fire Service College. The cemetery contains forty-seven war graves, belonging to airmen from the nearby aerodrome who died on active duty in the Second World War. The stones are in neat rows of white headstones of Portland stone, with roses planted at the graves. A stone wayside cross, incorporating a bronze sword, has been erected by the Commonwealth War Graves Commission.

Continuing on into the town, one passes over a railway bridge. Just before this, on the left, is Moreton's original cemetery and here the town's most distinguished son is buried. Born at Moreton in 1866, Thomas Sankey was created a Viscount in 1932. He was the son of Mr and Mrs Thomas Sankey, who ran a linen drapery in the town, and was educated at Oxford, where he obtained his degree in Arts and Law. He subsequently became a High Court judge, and when the Labour Party came to power in 1929 under Ramsey Macdonald, he fulfilled the position of Lord Chancellor. When a peerage was conferred on him he chose the title of Baron Sankey of Moreton-in-Marsh, becoming a Viscount in 1932. He died in 1948, aged eighty-two, and is buried in the lower cemetery at Moreton-in-Marsh. In 1935 he said 'I started at Moreton and I am going to finish at Moreton'. Towards the latter years of the twentieth century his grave became much neglected, but is now being taken care of in a manner that befits the town's most distinguished son.

Continuing on into the town centre, one arrives at the junction of Oxford Street (A44) and High Street (A429), where a curious tower will be seen. Dating from the sixteenth century, the Curfew Tower is one of the oldest buildings in the town.

It houses a bell, dated 1633, which was rung daily until 1860, and the lower room has been used as a lock-up for drunks. There is a story that one foggy night in the nineteenth century a gentleman named Sir Robert Fry was on his way back to Moreton-in-Marsh from London when he became lost on the common. Hearing the toll of the Curfew Bell in the distance, however, he regained his bearings and returned safely. In gratitude he left an endowment of £1 for winding the Curfew Clock and 10 shillings for ringing the bell. The bell was rung at 5 a.m. and 8 p.m. in summer, and 6 a.m. and 8 p.m. in winter. The last man to ring the curfew was William Webb, a man whose many tasks included the duties of parish constable. One day when placing a troublesome drunk in the lock-up, he sustained a broken leg; this is thought to have hastened his end, and he died in 1862, aged seventy-eight. More recently, the bell was rung to summon the local fire brigade to deal with fires.

Returning to wartime memorabilia, one is well-rewarded by a visit to the town's Wellington Aviation Museum, situated on the Bourton Road, on the west side of Moreton. Virtually a memorial to the Wellington bomber and RAF Moreton-in-Marsh, the museum has numerous artefacts of interest, including the actual tailplane of a bomber.

Across a field off the town's Hospital Road can be seen 'The Langate'. Marking the entrance of what is said to be the original path from Moreton-in-Marsh to Batsford, this stone gateway has an opening just over 4ft wide. The stone gateposts are 7ft high, with a stone wall some 8 yards long extending from one of the posts. The wall and posts are topped with capstones almost 3ft in length. The actual gate is purely functional, and of little note. In the early 1990s the wall was severely damaged by vandals, part of one section being pushed into an adjacent stream. Even so, the gate and entrance by foot to the Batsford estate are worth visiting.

Near the town's cricket ground on the Batsford Road, are the remains of a Roman camp. The camp lies on the north-west edge of Moreton-in-Marsh, the road from Moreton to Batsford actually cutting through it. Measuring about 165ft by 135ft, the earthwork consists of a single mound and ditch, most clearly visible in the field opposite the Cricket Lodge. It may have been a small outpost of the Roman town at nearby Dorn, or may pre-date it. It has been suggested that it may date from AD 43, and was a small Roman post used to maintain the submission of the local population.

Just off the road to Todenham, a couple of miles out of Moreton-in-Marsh, is the tiny village of Lower Lemington, which is today little more than a farm, a few cottages and a small Norman church. In fact, the approach off a lane leading from the Moreton-in-Marsh to Todenham road is through an open gateway, over a cattle grid and across a meadow. The church is of interest, retaining several Norman features in its structure, and its eighteenth-century fittings (including box pews and a three-decker pulpit) are particularly noteworthy.

During the Second World War the village was very close to RAF Moreton-in-Marsh, and it is said that in November 1941, when German high explosive bombs were dropped on the aerodrome, several fell into the marsh at nearby Brain's Coppice without detonating. If this tale is indeed true the bombs must be there still, deep in the marshy ground.

Todenham is the next village on the 'tour', some three miles north-east of Moreton-in-Marsh and close to the boundary between Gloucestershire and Warwickshire. It is one of my favourite Cotswold villages. To my eyes it is one of the most attractive, and I look back to how, as a policeman in the early 1980s, I used quite often to cycle from Moreton to Todenham. The station cycle was an old black model that was actually far too big for me, but by scooting it along and throwing a leg over the saddle, I was able to mount the machine. When I got there I would usually call at a cottage where I knew the owner, and would be given a drink of rough cider. It was fearsome stuff. Green in colour and sharp of taste, it was nevertheless always welcome sustenance and helped ensure my return journey went smoothly. I regarded this as all part of the 'community policing' ethos, though I have doubts as to whether the superintendent would have shared this view.

Sadly, Todenham has no shop or post office, but there is a very nice pub The Farrier's Arms. Nowadays a smart hostelry that serves excellent food, it is hard to believe that back in the 1970s it was the favoured 'hanging-out' place for bikers and Hell's Angels.

There are nice views across to 'Brailes Clump' on the top of the hill above Brailes, and it is very easy to get to nearby Shipston-on-Stour. There is a very fine Georgian manor house here, and the pretty church originates from the fourteenth century. The octagonal spire is especially handsome, and can be seen for miles around. Also, there is a thirteenth-century font, and outside on the south wall, a spooky-looking memorial tablet with skull and crossbones.

On land to the north of the village are the few remnants of Todenham Mill. The mill at Todenham was certainly in existence from at least the thirteenth century, and indeed there are various documentary references to it through the centuries that followed. It was still in use in the mid-1930s, the wheel being used to grind wheat and beans for cattle feed. It closed soon after, however, probably during the years of the Second World War. All that remains now are the mill pool, part of the race and the iron frame of the mill wheel. A footbridge nearby crosses Knee Brook and takes one into a field full of humps, bumps and peculiar outlines. These are the remains of the medieval village of Ditchford Frary. I am very fond of the area around the old mill. In the mid-1980s my then wife and I used to go there quite a lot. We would leave the car near The Farrier's Arms, follow the public footpath across the fields from Todenham to Ditchford Frary, then follow the rough track south-west to where it joins the road between the Fosse Way and Todenham, near Ditchford Mill. Just before the track joins the lane there are more peculiar undulations in the fields, this time forming the remains of the medieval village of Lower Ditchford. A short walk south-east takes one over a little stone bridge that crosses Knee Brook – from where I recall seeing dragonflies flying over the clear water below – and on past two railway cottages, before ascending the hill to Todenham. This is a very enjoyable circular walk, that has the added advantage of concluding at a welcoming hostelry.

In the sixteenth century the main street through Todenham ran west of the church, past Todenham Manor, and then east towards Burmington, in Warwickshire. From that road another road branched off towards Knee Brook, crossing it by means of a three-arch bridge. In 1895 this old road became more or less disused, the main road being diverted to Mitford Bridge, where Gloucestershire and Warwickshire meet, close to the junction with the A34 road from Chipping Norton to Shipston-on-Stour. Today the old road towards Knee Brook is little more than a track, used by horse-riders and walkers, but at the brook there is an old ford and the original bridge. The bridge is particularly photogenic and this part of Todenham is a lovely, unspoilt little haven.

In 1826 a tramway line was opened between Moreton-in-Marsh and Stratford-upon-Avon, with wagons being hauled along the line by horses, conveying coal and other commodities. It seems likely that the line was a somewhat rickety affair, though improvements and repairs had taken place by the time a branch to Shipston-on-Stour was completed in 1836. In 1886 the tramway line was re-laid for the use of locomotives. The passenger service from Moreton-in-Marsh to Shipston-on-Stour ceased in 1929, the line thereafter remaining in use for freight only. The speed limit along the branch line was just ten miles an hour, wagons of coal and fertiliser being transported twice each weekday. The railway was finally closed in 1960.

The line crossed Knee Brook near Todenham, and though the bridge has been gone for many years, the buttresses remain. A wander along the banks of the brook reveals the original stone footings to be still in place. It is a peaceful spot, easily reached by following the course of the old line from Wharf Cottage and Crossing Cottage.

Next to the lane that connects Todenham with the Fosse Way, at the point where it crosses the former railway line to Stratford and Shipston, there are the two railway cottages already mentioned. Wharf Cottage dates from the opening of the tramway

*The bridge over Knee Brook.*

in 1826, with Crossing Cottage next to it dating from when the line was re-laid in 1886 for steam locomotive use. Before the term 'station' came into use with regard to railways, the only term thought appropriate was 'wharf', which originates from the canal era. It is interesting to see the two cottages side by side.

To get to the village of Paxford is a simple matter. From the railway cottages, head north-west to join the Fosse Way, then turn right and, after a hundred yards or so, take the left turn into Galloping Lane. From this lane there are lovely, panoramic views towards Blockley and Aston Magna. About midway along the lane there is the start of a public footpath, which affords a pleasant walk of just over a mile to the nearby Warwickshire village of Stretton-on-Fosse. There happens to be a very good pub, The Plough, in this village, where it is possible to get a good snack or meal.

Paxford itself is an agreeable enough little village near the railway line from Oxford to Worcester. There is a level crossing and a brick works, which, though claimed as part of Blockley, is actually very much nearer Paxford. And there is a fine pub, The Churchill Arms, where excellent food can be had. It is very popular indeed, though, so parking can be a problem – for motorists and residents alike.

From Paxford, take the lane north to join the B4035 road until, after less than a mile, a crossroads is reached. Crossing this road takes one into May Lane, and thence to the village of Ebrington, a charming place with several thatched stone cottages and a good country inn, The Ebrington Arms. Until relatively recent times, Ebrington (pronounced 'Yubberton' by those who favour the rustic-sounding local dialect) had the unenviable reputation as home to rather more than the usual number of simpletons than is the case in most Cotswold villages. The tales of the 'Yubberton Yawnies' are well known in the Cotswolds, though these yarns are probably best appreciated by a particularly credulous audience.

You are high on the wolds now, and it is only a short drive to Hidcote Bartrim. For anyone interested in fine gardens, both Hidcote Manor and Kiftsgate Court merit visiting. Hidcote Manor Garden is a National Trust property and is probably one of the finest gardens in England. It is actually a series of delightful gardens separated by colourful hedges and mellow walls. Nearby, on a dramatic, steep hillside setting, Kiftsgate Court Garden, is another series of lovely interconnecting gardens. Begun in the 1920s, the gardens are continually evolving.

There is a particularly good view of the village of Mickleton, and beyond into neighbouring counties, from the lane between Hidcote Manor and Kiftsgate Court. This looks down over the wooded valley of Weeping Hollow where – according to folklore – the 'Mickleton Hooter' resides. This, apparently, is a ghost that howls and screeches, the rational explanation being that the funnel effect of the steep-sided valley sometimes amplifies natural sounds.

It is only about a mile down the hill into Mickleton. This village, lying beneath the northern edge of the Cotswolds, has almost as much in common with Warwickshire and the Vale of Evesham as with its native Gloucestershire. There is a mixture of architectural styles, with cottages of stone, brick, thatch and half-timber, and the village has several curiosities. On a small triangular green close to The Three Ways House Hotel is a memorial fountain, which consists of an arched niche under a gable and was designed in 1875 by William Burges, the architect of Cardiff Castle.

The Three Ways House Hotel has its own curiosity – in the form of 'The Pudding Club'. The club was formed at the hotel in 1985 'to prevent the demise of the traditional great British pudding'. Members of the club meet a couple of times each month and, after a main course, feast on a choice of seven puddings – ranging from favourites like Jam Roly Poly, to the more obscure Lord Randall's Pudding. The Pudding Club has been featured on radio and television programmes and has grown in popularity and reputation since it was formed.

The church, on the southern edge of the village, has a fine fourteenth-century tower and spire, and of particular note is a twelfth-century crucifix, over the north aisle chapel altar. It has a crudely carved figure of Christ on the Cross, with the carving repeated on the other side of the stone. Apparently, this was found in digging a grave by the porch and is thought originally to have been the head of a Norman churchyard cross.

As one follows the B4081 road between Mickleton and Chipping Campden one passes beneath the railway line from Oxford to Worcester. Nearby is Campden Tunnel, scene of the so-called 'Battle of Mickleton Tunnel' in 1851. During the driving of the tunnel a dispute over remuneration took place between the railway company and Robert Rudge-Marchant, the contractor engaged to complete the work, and he and his men stopped work. He posted guards to prevent his eviction but on 17 July 1851 the great engineer Isambard Kingdom Brunel arrived at the site with hundreds of navvies, determined to evict Marchant. The local magistrates had been warned, however, and Brunel found himself confronting not only Marchant's private army, but the local magistrates, supported by police armed with cutlasses. The Riot Act was read and the contending forces withdrew.

Brunel returned at 3 a.m. a day later, supported by an army of 200 navvies, and battle commenced against Marchant's men. A fierce fight followed, but more men arrived to support Brunel's army, Marchant finally finding himself up against a force of 2,000 navvies from Ireland and the Black Country. Resistance was hopeless and Marchant called for a truce, on the promise of an arbitrated settlement. The police subsequently arrived, supported by a detachment of troops from Coventry, but they were not required. There had been skirmishes and one account describes 'many broken heads and limbs', but thankfully there were no fatalities. It is a curious episode, and of the rail passengers who enter Campden Tunnel, there are probably few who realize they are passing over a battleground.

It is many years since a train stopped at Mickleton, but the village actually had its own halt on the railway line between 1937 and 1941. 'Mickleton Halt' was situated on an embankment close to the rail bridge that passes over the B4632 road to Broadway, but all that remains of the halt today are some concrete steps that led up to it, together with a small gate.

It is a little over three miles from Mickleton, along the A46, to Saintbury. A village cross stands at the foot of the hill that leads up to the village, said to mark the point where funeral processions rested before ascending the hill to the church. The head of the cross is not earlier than 1848, but the shaft may date from the fourteenth century.

After passing several very attractive stone cottages and houses, one reaches the village Church of St Nicholas, with its slender spire and fine views across into Worcestershire and the Vale of Evesham. Inside there are eighteenth-century box pews of note, and on the exterior south wall there is a carved Anglo-Saxon sundial, with the day divided into eight tides of three hours each. Unusually, the rays are carved in relief, rather than scratched in stone. Also of interest is a crudely carved figure, with stumps for legs, in the splay of the window of the south wall. This is thought to date from the eleventh century.

*The entrance to the Ernest Wilson Memorial Garden at Chipping Campden.*

A curious sight can be had after dark as one approaches the village from the Chipping Campden direction. Worcestershire and the Vale of Evesham are spread out ahead, and there in the plain, about four miles distant, is a series of extremely bright lights that would not look out of place in a movie such as *Close Encounters of the Third Kind*. There are several small passing places on the lane, from where the lights may be seen. Incongruous in this rural setting, the lights will surely appear curious to anyone unfamiliar with their source. They are actually the lights of Long Lartin prison at South Littleton – a top security establishment that houses a number of notorious criminals, murderers and violent offenders.

However, daylight is recommended for the next 'stop'. Undoubtedly one of the loveliest towns in the Cotswolds, Chipping Campden has a particularly attractive High Street, with a number of beautiful houses along its length. I have always regarded the town as the most attractive and unspoilt in the area. It was an important wool trading centre in the fourteenth and fifteenth centuries – the church, with its handsome pinnacled tower, is one of the finest of the Cotswold 'wool' churches. The handsome Market Hall, built in 1627 by Sir Baptist Hicks, the first Viscount Campden, and now owned by The National Trust, is another notable feature. Earlier, in 1612, he built the fine row of almshouses near the church. Opposite the almshouses is a curious stone-lined pit, dating from the early nineteenth century. It was used for washing carts and soaking their wheels, and replaced a pond that had existed earlier at the bottom of Church Street.

Next to the church are two impressive gatehouses, originally the entrance to Campden House, which Sir Baptist Hicks built for himself. Once a notable architectural feature of the town, it was of ornate Italian style. In 1645, however, as the English Civil War came close to ending, the third Viscount Campden set fire to the house, rather than let it fall into Puritan hands. That, at least, is the story. It is thought more probable that drunken Royalist soldiers torched it before fleeing. This was just thirty years after it had been built. Almost nothing remains of the actual house, but an area of uneven ground near the church shows traces of medieval fish ponds. A short distance away is a stone gateway standing isolated in a meadow. Known as 'Lady Juliana's Gateway', this stands at what was once the bottom of the Campden House garden.

There are several other unusual features worth seeking out. A lovely little oasis away from the bustle can be seen at the Ernest Wilson Memorial Garden, just off Leysbourne, a little to the north of the High Street. Once part of the vicarage grounds, the garden was opened in 1984 to commemorate Chipping Campden's notable botanist. Ernest Wilson was born in the town on 15 February 1876, where he spent part of his childhood before moving to live in Birmingham, where he began his career at the Botanical Gardens. He travelled to China and the Far East, collecting thousands of plants, before becoming keeper of the Arnold Arboretum at the USA's Harvard University. Unfortunately, he never returned to live in Chipping Campden – he and his wife were tragically killed in a car crash in 1930. The memorial garden has many plants first introduced to Britain by Wilson.

All of the other curious sites are outside the town. To start with, there is an interesting guide post at the junction of the A44 and B4081 roads to the south of Chipping Campden. The direction sign is very tall, the directions to Oxford, Warwick, Worcester and Gloucester indicated by the hands of four wrought iron arms. It is believed to stand on the site of a gallows, thought to be where the unfortunate victims of 'The Campden Wonder' were hanged in 1660. A Mr Izod from the parish of Chipping Campden erected the sign in 1669 – the present wooden shaft is believed to be the latest in a long line of replacements, the original post having been broader and somewhat less tall. The signpost has always been regarded important and in 1675 received mention in Ogilby's *Britannia*.

Left: *The Kiftsgate Stone.*

Below: *Sir Baptist Hicks's 'conduit house'.*

In a little clearing in a wood next to the lane between Broadway and Mickleton, to the west of Chipping Campden, stands the Kiftsgate Stone. Only 3ft in height, and clearly ancient, the traditions that surround it are interesting. *Kifts* is believed to derive from the Old English *cyft*, meaning meeting or conference. Thus 'Kiftsgate' could mean 'gate where meetings are held'. The stone does indeed mark what was once a moot place where local people met to administer justice, discuss business and hold festivals. In Domesday Book the area around the stone was called the Cheftsihat Hundred and meetings of the Kiftsgate Hundred took place at the stone.

As one approaches the town from the south, on the B4081 road leading down Westington Hill, one sees a small stone building on the roadside. Squat and windowless, it has no obvious purpose, but was in fact erected by Sir Baptist Hicks in 1612 over a natural spring, from which water was conducted to a fountain or standpipe in front of Chipping Campden's almshouses. Sir Baptist's 'conduit house' is a fairly basic but solidly built structure, with a small doorway giving access to a semi-underground chamber containing a stone trough, which still runs with clear water.

Annual games known as the 'Cotswold Olympics' take place each May on the top of an 800ft hill to the west of the town. The games, which originally included 'sports' as diverse as throwing the hammer, standing on the hands of kneeling men, and shin kicking, were instituted by Captain Robert Dover in the reign of King James I. The games were apparently very popular, taking place for some 200 years, until the regular attendance of 'the scum of the Black Country' – as stated by Francis Duckworth in his 1908 book *The Cotswolds* – brought about their end in 1852. The games were revived as an annual event in the 1960s, however, and continue to attract people from a wide area – though no major 'scum' problems are encountered. A highlight of the day is when, at the end of the games, a procession bearing lighted torches parades down the hill into the square at Chipping Campden, where music and festivities continue throughout the evening. I well remember performing duty at the games, and afterwards in Campden's square, in the early 1980s. It was 'traditional' for the policemen to partake of a little liquid refreshment at the nearby Lygon Arms when their duties were concluded and I think it safe to say that afterwards they were of at least as merry a temperament as most of the town's revellers!

The hill on which the games take place is called Dover's Hill and is owned by the National Trust, the outline of an Iron Age hillfort still clearly visible. A popular site for walkers, a viewpoint on the summit gives fine views across the Vale of Evesham and beyond to the Malvern Hills. Also, a monument of about 1934 commemorating Captain Robert Dover (1582-1652) can be seen near the entrance gate to the hill. Sadly, this has in recent years been somewhat defaced.

Finally, about a mile out of Chipping Campden, just off the B4081 road to Mickleton, there is a seventeenth-century house and garden where, until recent years, time seemed to have stood still. Norton House, owned by the Earl and Countess of Harrowby, who live in Staffordshire, was surrounded by woodland and semi-wild gardens, remaining uninhabited and virtually untouched for almost a quarter of a century. After a colourful history, the house was set alight in 1741 by its owner, Sir William Keyte, who had suffered a catalogue of self-inflicted financial and personal misfortunes. Keyte perished in the blaze, but an adjoining farmhouse escaped damage, becoming known as Burnt Norton. In 1934 the poet T.S. Eliot, who was visiting a friend in Chipping Campden, called at Burnt Horton. He was so inspired by it that he wrote *Burnt Norton*, one of *The Four Quartets*, making particular reference to a dry pool, which last held water in 1900. The house is now lived in by Viscount Sandon and the garden has been tidied and improved. The property is private but may be visited by written application to Viscount Sandon at Burnt Norton Hall, Chipping Campden.

There are numerous good pubs and hotels in the town, and various excellent shops and businesses. The Volunteer Inn, at the west end of the High Street, is probably one of the best pubs, serving a good choice of local real ales. The town becomes full with cars in the summer months, of course, so a visit out of season may be preferred. There will be many in Chipping Campden who remember how the town became virtually 'medieval' again for a day in 1971. The Italian film director, Pasolini, used the High Street and Market Hall as the setting for part of his film of Chaucer's *Canterbury Tales*. The roads were covered with sand and straw, modern signs were covered up and numerous extras wore period costume.

The next village to be visited is not much more than a good stone's throw from Chipping Campden. Broad Campden is a charming little village, with quiet lanes and thatched cottages, and has a Norman chapel that is today a private residence, shielded from prying eyes by a high wall and hedge. Very welcoming, though, is the village inn, The Baker's Arms. It always has a selection of real ales and serves very good food, while retaining a 'village pub' atmosphere.

It was when passing through Broad Campden some time ago that I noticed a very visible indication of 'ridge and furrow' strip-field farming in meadows off the lane towards Paxford. These remnants of a bygone age are very common in the Cotswolds – and, indeed, throughout much of England – and look particularly striking when shadows are cast upon the furrows by the evening sun. This 'ridge and furrow' effect occurred when in medieval times villagers owned and farmed individual strips in very large open fields. Teams of oxen were used to plough these strips, creating the great ridges still visible today. This medieval form of farming died out in the eighteenth century, when the open fields became enclosed into the smaller, compact fields common until recent years. If a good example of 'ridge and furrow' is sought, it would be difficult to find a more picturesque setting.

In order to make this 'tour' around the North Cotswolds at least vaguely circular it is necessary to travel around six miles to the next location. After going back to Chipping Campden, then taking the B4081 road up Westington Hill and on to the A44 road to Evesham, the minor road to Snowshill should be followed. And Snowshill is certainly worth the effort. This lovely hillside village has a number of very pretty houses and cottages, mainly grouped around the churchyard and village green. Best-known, however, is the village's curious manor house. Snowshill Manor dates back to around 1500, but became what it is today after Charles Wade moved into this odd-looking Tudor house in 1919, using it to store his ever-increasing collection of bicycles, Samurai armour, toys, timepieces and, well, just about anything. In time his collection became so huge that he moved out of the house to live in an outbuilding in the garden. He was reputed to have been a student of the occult, and, easily overlooked in the garden, is a horoscope carved in the stone of a path. More sinister, and not generally open to the public, is an attic room known as 'the witches' garret', which is full of necromantic paraphernalia. Wade eventually moved to live in the West Indies, giving the house and contents to the National Trust. The house is crammed with bizarre exotica, and anyone interested in curiosities is unlikely to be disappointed by a visit.

Near the village are several woods. Littleworth Wood is on the Cotswold Way and has a small car park near its north-western corner from where one may walk to the village of Stanton. Fortunately, both Snowshill and Stanton have pubs that serve local Donnington Ales – The Snowshill Arms and The Mount Inn, respectively – to help fortify oneself before and after any walk.

Welshman's Hedge Wood, near the village, is remembered by some for a very different reason. In 1967 a doctor working in general practice at Moreton-in-Marsh became romantically involved with a local woman. Both she and the doctor were already married, and the affair became something of a local talking point. But worse was to come. One afternoon the doctor went to the woman's home and asked her to come away with him, and, when she refused, he drew a sawn-off shotgun and shot her dead. He left the scene and was found dead in his car at Welshman's Hedge Wood that evening, having taken a fatal overdose of drugs. The event made the national press, of course, and for a while Moreton became a centre of attention. Now, in the following century, the bitter tragedy is rarely recalled, but for those involved in the case, Welshman's Hedge Wood holds significance.

Taddington is a couple of miles south of Snowshill, past Welshman's Hedge Wood.

There is very little at this small upland hamlet, other than a few houses and a fine seventeenth-century barn. The main significance of the place is that the picturesque River Windrush rises in a field here. A little to the east of the hamlet there is a track – shown as 'unsuitable for motors' – that leads from Taddington towards the prehistoric Buckle Street. Following this for a short distance leads one to a bridge called 'Dirty Bridge'. The track is very wet at this point, caused by the fledgling River Windrush seeping onto the road. A few fields away a modern building can be seen – this is 'Field Barn' – and it is in a field near this dwelling that the spring rises to form the river. Bubbling beneath a large flat stone, and trickling into a pool surrounded by reeds, this is the source of the famous river. It goes on to meander through the hills and fields to flow beneath the little bridges at Bourton-on- the- Water and on to Oxfordshire, before running into the Thames at Newbridge.

The track from the hamlet towards Buckle Street is itself well worth taking a wander along. Very little used other than by walkers and people on horseback, the verges are a haven for the kinds of wild flowers one seldom sees on the roadside today. There are pleasant views over the fields towards Pewit Hill and I fondly recall how, years ago, I used occasionally to come here late in the evening with a lady companion to watch the hills and fields bathed in moonlight.

Less than a mile from the source of the River Windrush at Taddington is Cutsdean, thought by some to have taken its name from an Anglo-Saxon chief named Cod, becoming 'Cod's dene'. The hill country round about became known as 'Cod's wold', or Cotswold. The theory cannot be proven, of course, but it does seem quite plausible. The village is centred on a wide green, and owing to its exposed position, can at times look a little bleak. Its church is a very small building, curiously situated in a farmyard, and was originally fourteenth-century, but was substantially rebuilt in 1863. According to most guides on the Cotswolds, it is 'without interest', but I found it rather appealing. It is to be hoped that the villagers support their church.

Beside the road near Manor Farm is a Grade II listed stone sheep wash that was uncovered by Cotswold Wardens in 1993. It had been full of mud and was almost completely overgrown. When the wash was in operation, sheep would have been bathed in the deep end of the banjo-shaped trough before being allowed to escape up the exit ramp. Made of local Cotswold stone, the trough is 12ft wide and 5ft deep, and would have been filled with water from a spring, which rises at the back of a cottage opposite the wash. At the deepest end of the trough is an oak sluice gate, which would have been released to let the water out. The age of the structure is uncertain, and villagers say it was last used in 1920. By the 1930s it was being used as a rubbish dump, but in 1978 volunteers from the village began clearing it out, the work being completed some years later by the Wardens. Certainly it is an unusual feature and is worth visiting.

Within easy walking distance, should you fancy stretching your legs, is Ford. There isn't very much at this little village – which is situated on the B4077 road to Stow-on-the-Wold – but there is an excellent pub, The Plough. It is a 'real' Cotswold pub, serving Mr Arkell's fine Donnington Ales, but has the added attraction of serving very good food.

Next take the B4077 north-west out of Ford for a short distance, then take the lane on the left towards Farmcote. This is a tiny hamlet with a handsome house, which is close to a barn and farm buildings thought to have been a grange of Hailes Abbey. Alone in a field a short walk away is the little Church of St Faith. Standing above Hailes, with fine views towards Bredon Hill and the Malvern Hills, this church has a Norman nave, and Tudor south door and windows. Sixteenth-century oak benches, Elizabethan effigies and a Jacobean two-decker pulpit and Laudian altar rail add to the building's charm and interest. Arthur Mee, in his *King's England: Gloucestershire* says: '…who can forget this lonely place on a lovely hill?' Remote and unspoilt, and in a beautiful setting, this is a particularly suitable place in which to rest and reflect.

On the hill above Farmcote is an Iron Age promontory fort known as Beckbury Camp where in the north-west corner there is an ancient and curious stone pillar, known as 'Cromwell's Seat'. What its purpose was is not known, but legend says that from it King Henry VIII's Commissioner, Thomas Cromwell, watched the destruction of Hailes Abbey in the valley below. The fort itself is quite small, but has a well-preserved bank on the east and south, which rises 5ft above the interior. The monument is accessible on foot only.

A walk south from Beckbury Camp towards Farmcote and Guiting Wood takes one past two places where strip lynchets are visible. These are cultivation terraces on the side of a hill and are usually Anglo-Saxon or medieval and are the visible evidence of a special kind of ploughing, where the heavy plough created horizontal terraces on the slopes. On sloping ground, the plough was naturally driven horizontally along the hillside rather than against the hill. Over time, the effect was for the furrow slices to be deposited downhill, until the strips eventually became level terraces, with the balks between them becoming steep banks, usually termed lynchets.

Following the lane from Farmcote and on through Guiting Wood towards Temple Guiting leads one to some curiosities of a completely different kind. At the start of a grassy track leading to Guiting Power two slabs of limestone have at some time been placed at the beginning of the track – presumably to keep vehicles from entering. One of the slabs has been fashioned into the shape of a frog or toad, apparently sitting on the grass. The rock is of local limestone, and being fairly soft, is starting to show significant signs of wear. Up the hill towards Temple Guiting, and

*The stone tortoise at Temple Guiting.*

close to Lousehill Plantation, are similarly carved rocks, this time in the form of a hare, tortoise and grasshopper. Locals say the rocks were carved in the early 1990s by a young traveller named Zebedee, who had set up camp nearby. What became of Zebedee is not known, though there is some suggestion that he moved to the Stroud area.

Kineton is just half a mile south of Temple Guiting. This is a nice little hamlet, but other than a welcoming pint of Donnington Ale at The Half Way House pub in its centre, there is not a great deal to attract the visitor. The River Windrush flows through the eastern fringes of Kineton and there are a couple of fords that one can negotiate. Be warned, though. The northerly ford is really quite deep and can only be safely negotiated in a large four-wheel drive vehicle. This ford has a clapper bridge next to it for the use of pedestrians. Both fords are highly photogenic, the Windrush being lined with trees at this point.

A road running west out of Kineton, known as Critchford Lane, is a very pretty gated lane that leads to a ford through Castlett Stream, before the lane leads onward to Guiting Power. No one would describe this lane as busy, so I remember with some amusement being tasked, back in the 1980s, to stop traffic, in order for a camera crew to film unimpeded as a car roared through the ford. Needless to say, there was no traffic for me to hold up, but I recall watching with interest as a number of adders basked on the warm surface of the lane, apparently oblivious to my presence.

The neat stone village of Guiting Power is very attractive indeed, the cluster of mellow stone buildings looking particularly charming when seen on a clear day from the hill above the village. It has two excellent pubs – The Farmer's Arms and The Hollow Bottom, both of which are popular with visitors and locals alike.

In the rural beauty of such a place one little expects to find the remains of an industrial enterprise. Yet in the early nineteenth century at Fox Hill the headquarters of the Stone Pipe Company were engaged in the production of water pipes from solid stone, utilising a process patented in 1805 by one Sir George Wright. Such was the success of the company that there were plans to extend a railway from the works at Guiting Power to link up with the tramway at Leckhampton, on the edge of Cheltenham. It was not to be, however, and the inadequacies of their product led to the collapse of the Stone Pipe Company. Today, in the lane that descends westwards from Naunton to Guiting, via Tally Ho Farm, evidence of this former works is still visible in the shape of broken pipes in field walls that surround the tree-covered works by the lane.

At Bemborough Farm, above the village, visitors can see the Cotswold Farm Park. Opened in 1970, it forms a large collection of ancient and rare breeds of farm animals, such as Old Gloucester cows, Gloucester Old Spot pigs and Cotswold sheep. Kept in a natural farm environment, these animals are protected and nurtured in a thoroughly professional way, the park having developed into a unique attraction.

Hinchwick, the next recommended stop, is about five miles north-east of Guiting. There is actually very little at Hinchwick, which is one of its main attractions. In the Cotswolds there is rarely a sense of being far from civilisation, but when approached on the little unclassified lane from the A424, one passes through a wooded valley with a series of lakes just visible through the trees. If one pauses at the roadside here it is easy to imagine the haunting sound of duelling banjos echoing through the woods, and there is a real sense of being in 'hillbilly country'. That isn't really the case, of course, and all too quickly one passes through the wooded valley and comes upon the manor house and its nearby cottages. But, as one of the truly 'secret' villages in the Cotswolds, Hinchwick should not be missed.

Above Hinchwick Manor is Bourton Downs – a little-known area of natural Cotswold grassland. This can be explored by public rights-of-way.

About a mile south of Hinchwick is the village of Condicote. If one enters this village off the A436 road from Stow-on-the-Wold, the first real sign of habitation is a collection of farm buildings of stone, near two particularly blind bends. Ahead is an old wind pump, and various agricultural implements lay spread around the fields next to the road. Occasionally a sheepdog wanders from the buildings to bark at passing vehicles. Some might say all this is rather scruffy and untidy, but I say it is a very welcome sight. At last – signs of genuine rural life in a rural Cotswold village.

After passing this rural scene it will be found that Condicote is a quiet village centred on a large green of rough grass, surrounded by a stone wall. On the western side of the green is a spring marked by a cross, though only the socket and three steps remain from the original fourteenth century structure. Restoration work took place in 1864, the cross being replaced in 1888 with one from the church. The water from the spring is reputed to have healing properties. From this spring a pump pipes water into a trough on the green, the well beneath the cross being for the use of the villagers, while the trough on the green is for more general use. An inscription on the cross is now almost illegible, but in the 1928 book *Ancient Wells, Springs and Holy Wells of Gloucestershire* by R.C. Skyring Walters, it is shown as:

THIS WELL IS RESERVED FOR THE
DOMESTIC PURPOSES OF THE
INHABITANTS OF THIS PARISH:
FOR ALL OTHER USES, RECOURSE
TO THE PUMP AND TROUGH IS
RESPECTFULLY SUGGESTED.
SEE RESOLUTION OF VESTRY,
MARCH 16TH 1865.

In ancient times Condicote must have been regarded as a place of importance. Near Luckley Farm, between Longborough and Condicote, is a Bronze Age cemetery containing at least nine round barrows. Most of these tumuli are contained within Hull Plantations, which has led to better preservation than has been the case at Cow Common Cemetery, near Lower Swell. Also, there is no obvious sign that they have been interfered with, though it is quite likely that these tombs contain cremations. Additionally, and somewhat better known than the cemetery, is Condicote's henge. Unfortunately for those on foot or in a motor vehicle, the site – much reduced over the past 100 years or so – needs to be seen from the air for its size and shape to be fully appreciated. Even so, it is worth taking a glance at what remains of the banks. The henge comprises of two circular ditches with a single bank between them. The site has been archaeologically examined, with the discovery of Beaker-related pottery, radiocarbon dating showing that the site was constructed before 18 BC. The actual purpose of the henge is not certain, but it is thought that it was used for religious ceremonies. The road from Longborough into the village cuts through the middle of the monument, but for the casual observer, the remains of the embankment can be seen near the small village hall building.

The Romans knew Condicote, too. The Roman road Ryknild Street – known

*The well cross at Condicote, c. 1900.*

locally as Condicote Lane – runs north-south past the village, on its way from Bourton-on-the-Water to Etocetum, near Wall in Staffordshire. Visible as a rough track it can be seen on the right, opposite the left turn into the village, as one approaches from the B4077 road. The village of Longborough, a couple of miles to the north-east, seems to have it all: a fine church with a handsome thirteenth-century tower; attractive stone cottages and houses; a good village school; a friendly and very useful village shop and post office, and a 'real' Cotswold pub serving locally brewed ales. Until a few years ago, too, the village had a resident eccentric – in the form of 'Bert', a gentleman who lived with his pony in a shed on the allotments. An early riser, Bert would frequently be heard at the crack of dawn, blowing a hunting horn as a kind of reveille to the village. Bert died some years ago, and though Longborough is probably quieter at dawn than it used to be, his bizarre behaviour is fondly recalled by many.

The church is of interest for several reasons. Not only is the tower very imposing, but the fourteenth-century embattled south transept is really very beautiful. The font is early fourteenth century and has an octagonal bowl. It is of special significance for me because my own two dear sons were baptized here. Below the window of the south transept is the effigy of a knight, his head supported by fourteenth-century winged angels. The slab on which the effigy rests was originally the

*The effigy of an unknown knight at Longborough.*

lid of the coffin in which the knight was buried – the effigy is actually older than the Chapel in which it lies. Of unknown identity, this knight is thought perhaps to be connected with the great house at Banks Fee.

The village pub, The Coach and Horses, overlooks the little green and war memorial. It is strictly a pub for drink only – do not expect food more exotic than crisps or peanuts – but is nevertheless very friendly and welcoming. It has flagstone floors; there is a dartboard in regular use, and there is a log fire in winter. Connie, the landlady, has been in residence for more than thirty years, serving ales from the nearby Donnington Brewery, and there is no reason to anticipate any significant change in the near future. Even so, those who seek a genuinely traditional Cotswold pub are advised to pay a visit sooner rather than later. On the other side of the village, on the road towards Stow-on-the-Wold, there is a well known as the Ash Well at the side of the road. A lane leads past this well and down a slope across fields to nearby Donnington. Fairly close by, on the hill above the lane, is a fine house of around 1760 called Banks Fee. In an obscure publication of 1800, *The Muse in Gloucestershire*, the author T. Horde describes how the owner of the house, a Mr Scott, had improved the gardens, laying out plantations and a deer park. He goes on to say:

> … Down in the bottom, ponds, with fish, we find,
> In number plenteous, excellent in kind …

About midway between the villages of Longborough and Donnington one passes fairly near to an attractive lake that is much populated by wild ducks, and fish that are 'plenteous' in number. The fish are, quite probably, 'excellent in kind', too.

Fine gardens are to be seen at several of the villages next on the agenda. Just off the lane between Longborough and Bourton-on-the-Hill, is Sezincote. There has not been an actual village at Sezincote since medieval times, but the magnificent Sezincote House is itself very interesting indeed. Situated on the hill between Moreton-in-Marsh and Longborough, it is a particularly fascinating house and garden, much in the Indian style. The Indian connection dates back to 1795, when the estate was bought by Colonel John Cockerell on his return from Bengal. He employed a brother, Samuel Pepys Cockerell – an architect who was surveyor to the East India Company – to build him a house in the Indian manner. Cockerell worked with artist Thomas Daniell, who had just returned from ten years in India, and the house and garden we see today was created. A mixture of Hindu and Muslim detail, Sezincote is a unique example of the architecture of Akbar – Moghul ruler of India from 1556 to 1605.

Particularly striking, and visible from quite some distance away, is the roof dome. This is characteristic of Muslim architecture – a symbol of peace and tranquillity – and shows the Persian influence. The dome was originally burnished copper but is now coated with verdigris. Following a visit to Sezincote by the Prince Regent in 1806, it became the inspiration for the Indianization of the Brighton Pavilion.

The Indian influence is also much in evidence in the garden. A bridge is decorated with Brahmin sacred bulls, and near a pool and fountain is a temple in which there is a statue of Surya, the sun god. Behind the greenhouse is the Wellington Memorial, almost hidden by trees. Beautifully planted with bamboos, maples, cedars and a host of exotic plants, Sezincote is very much worthy of a visit. The garden is open on Thursday and Friday, and Bank Holiday afternoons.

The next 'stop' is Bourton-on-the-Hill, not much more than half a mile north. It is easy to pass through this village on the A44 road from Moreton-in-Marsh to Evesham without fully appreciating its beauty. Negotiation of the steep hill and narrow road requires concentration, and the traveller is doing well if he manages to glance at the stone cottages on either side of the road. Certainly drivers are unlikely to notice one of the village's most interesting features, the disused quarries at the top of the hill leading out of the village. The quarries, opened up in 1853, are situated between the turnings to Longborough and Blockley, the distinctive yellow stone quarried from them being used for a number of local buildings, including the hospital and Redesdale Hall at Moreton-in-Marsh. Stone was taken to London, too, to make rockeries at Buckingham Palace and Kew Gardens and by

*Mason's Cave at Bourton-on-the-Hill.*

the early twentieth century some thirty workers, including three banker masons, were employed at Bourton quarries. Several caves were made in the quarries for the banker masons, one of which can still be seen at the junction of the A44 and the lane to Longborough. The First World War saw much of the local workforce leave to join the forces, however, and the quarries closed in 1915. Over the decades that have followed they have become picturesque havens for wildlife, flora and fauna, the rocky quarry faces appearing particularly striking as the stone glints when the sun's rays filter between the branches of the trees.

A little way down the hill towards Moreton-in-Marsh is an excellent pub, The Horse and Groom, noted for the excellence of its cuisine. Continuing towards the foot of the hill, one finds the lovely Bourton House Garden. Displaying numerous interesting and delightful features, including an eighteenth century raised walk, the garden and its magnificent tithe barn (built in 1570) is certainly worth a visit.

However, returning to the village's curiosities, we will find a fairly dense wood, known locally as 'The Camp', just off the A424 to the west. During the years of the Second World War, before the wood existed, a camp for German prisoners of war stood on the site. The camp has long since been dismantled and removed, though concrete roadways that ran between the buildings still exist and substantial piles of broken-up concrete spread throughout the wood indicate the previous existence of some fairly large structures.

When permitted, the POWs turned their hands to the creation of model buildings, fashioned from stone and concrete. Surprisingly, a few of these structures survive today, though their presence is not widely known of. Almost in the middle of the wood a small cottage can be seen, bearing the inscription 'Weiler Muhle. A few yards away a castle, complete with four towers, stands close to a large house. These buildings stand about 3ft high and are in fairly good condition, though none has a roof. Apparently, there have been other buildings in the wood, including one that was made from tobacco tins. The wood is privately owned by the Sezincote Estate, from whom permission should be sought to view the models. Additionally, it is said that there are a number of very deep, uncovered manholes in the wood. This is, of course, a very good reason to resist any urge to trespass.

Another part of the Bourton-on-the-Hill parish of particular interest is the beauty spot known as the 'Jockey Stables Pool'. When travelling on the unclassified road from the A44 towards Snowshill, one descends a steep slope, with a roadside pool at the foot of the hill. A lane next to the pool leads to Far Upton Wold and a small group of dwellings known as the 'Jockey Stable Cottages'. It is a particularly peaceful spot, a stream leading from the pool and under a little stone bridge. Though this beauty spot seems to be rarely frequented nowadays, it must have once been quite a popular place, for until the 1980s there used to be a roadside sign, which read: 'let no one say it and say it to your shame, that all was beauty here until you came'. The sign has now disappeared, and the grass at the poolside has a somewhat unkempt appearance. Even so, it remains a tranquil and lovely place.

To get to Blockley, the next village on the 'tour', one should take the B4479 road, which leads off the A44 near the old quarry at Bourton-on-the-Hill. There is much to see in Blockley, and though it has been termed a 'secret' village in some publications, it is really quite large and not very far from the main Oxford to Worcester road. Depending on which side you approach from, it can look positively lovely (from the Bourton-on-the-Hill side) or relatively unattractive (from the Paxford side).

In the early years of the nineteenth century the village enjoyed prosperity when silk mills working on the brook that runs through Blockley provided employment for some 500 people. The mills have long since closed, but the village retains an unspoilt charm, with its pretty bowling green and steep terraces and streets. The Church of St Peter and St Paul is as good a place as any to begin one's search for curiosities. The impressive tower was built in 1725, though the chancel is late Norman, its walls adorned with various memorials. A couple of these bear sculptures of doom and forboding, one carved skull lending its memorial a particularly macabre air. On leaving the church and heading into Bell Lane, one sees 'Bell

*The prisoners' model castle at Bourton-on-the-Hill.*

Cottage'. Readers will not be surprised to learn that this was formerly an inn – The Bell. It closed in 1970 and was converted into private dwellings, building work leading to the discovery of seven human skeletons lying beneath the floorboards of the public rooms! Carbon dating revealed the probable date of the skeletons to be AD 840 – substantially older than The Bell inn building. It is probable that this was a Christian burial (at one time the churchyard extended well beyond its present limits), the original builders of the inn disturbing the bones as little as possible when they found them.

Rising steeply from Bell Lane is Bell Bank, a lane barely wide enough to permit the passage of a vehicle. Near the top of this lane is Blockley's 'Little Village Hall' – not to be confused with the larger and far less intimate St George's Hall, in Park Road. The Little Village Hall is delightful, full of character and well worth booking if you intend holding a small function in the village. In 1792 the hall was built by the Reverend Elisha Smith as a Baptist Meeting House, and in 1925 his descendants presented it to the people of Blockley as a Village Hall. It was thoroughly renovated and overhauled in 1995 and today stands as a most unusual and charming stone-built Georgian building of distinction.

If one walks along the High Street from Bell Lane, south towards an inn named The Crown, the road forming School Lane drops sharply to the left. At the foot of this hill is Mill Dene Garden, the lovely two-and-a-half-acre garden of a restored watermill. The garden is intimate and individual, with a tranquil mill-pond that is frequented by kingfishers and moorhens. This is another of those fine Cotswold gardens that merits a visit.

A walk along the narrow High Street, past The Crown and beyond to Dovedale Woods, provides one with a lovely view of the little houses that stand on the steep bank above Blockley Brook. It is difficult to believe now, but this part of the village had a reputation for lawlessness in the nineteenth century, and in 1878 an over-zealous local policeman was lucky to escape with his life after his attentions at The Crown led a rioting mob to chase him, drag him from his house and set about him. Taking care to avoid any baying mob that may appear, one finds the footway rises above the level of the road as one continues along the High Street. A short distance past the High Street's junction with Chapel Lane a fountain called 'Russell Spring' can be seen, set into the wall at the roadside opposite Malvern Mill. Clear water flows from the mouth of a lion, beautifully sculpted. Apparently, the water originally fell into a stone trough, the spring being much improved in 1830 by Lucy Russell, who operated Malvern Mill. The spring was completely rebuilt after the 1937 coronation, with the addition of the inscription:

WATER

FROM THE

LIVING ROCK

GOD'S PRECIOUS GIFT TO MAN

In 1994 a proposal to bottle and sell water from the spring caused protests in the village, though the idea was soon abandoned, the spring water remaining freely available to all.

A little further along the High Street stands Rock Cottage, where 'The Prophetess' Joanna Southcott lived as a guest between 1804 and 1814. Variously regarded as deluded, mad, or a visionary, she had begun writing down prophecies in 1792 and received much attention because of her belief that she would bear Shiloh, the second Messiah. At her death in 1814 she left more than sixty 'books' of prophesy, some of which described how she was visited by Satan and dreamt of fires in the sky. Incredibly, she became the focus of a large cult, her supporters forming 'The Panacea Society', which owns housing near London's Embankment. Rock Cottage was more or less destroyed by fire in 1971, but has since been restored.

Continuing along the High Street, past Day's Lane and on towards Dovedale Woods, yet another building connected with a curious tale stands back from the road. Fish Cottage has a little pool in its front garden, home to a pet trout in the nineteenth century. Apparently, the trout was very tame but was cruelly killed by a drunken neighbour in 1885. The fish's owner placed a headstone on its grave, the epitaph reading:

IN MEMORY
OF THE OLD FISH

UNDER THE SOIL
THE OLD FISH DO LIE
TWENTY YEARS HE LIVED
AND THEN DID DIE
HE WAS SO TAME
YOU UNDERSTAND
HE WOULD COME AND
EAT OUT OF OUR HAND

Died April 20th 1885. Aged 20 years.

For many years the memorial remained *in situ* but has now been placed inside a glass cabinet attached to the exterior wall of the cottage. This is private property, so permission should be sought before attempting to view the memorial.

Beyond Fish Cottage the source of Blockley Brook can be seen in Dovedale Woods, which stand at the end of the High Street (itself having become no more than a track at this point). This picturesque brook, such a key feature of Blockley's history, once ran the wheels of up to twelve mills in the village. Close to the source, and just below Dovedale House, is an artificial lake with a waterfall. In the 1880s parts of the village were supplied with electric light, created by a dynamo that was run by a water-wheel on the lake. Indeed, it has often been claimed that Blockley was the first village in the country to have electric light.

To see the village's next curiosities one needs to take a couple of short journeys. First, off the road to Bourton-on-the-Hill and up a rough track, stands Park Farm. To the front of the farmhouse is a medieval fish pond, and on the hill to the back of the farm, are a couple of pillow mounds. Blockley's Lord of the Manor was in those days the Bishop of Worcester, and 'the Bishop's Park' roughly corresponded with the land today forming Park Farm. The fish pond would originally have had several species of fish in it to provide a useful source of food when fresh meat became scarce in winter. The pillow mounds may at first glance appear to be barrows, and mounds such as these have indeed been the subject of much speculation. More common in the south of England, pillow mounds are now generally regarded as

*The medieval fish pond at Blockley.*

artificial rabbit warrens, the rabbits being used for their fur and as a source of food. Before departing, enjoy the view of Blockley from Park Farm. At the time of writing, the farmhouse is occupied by local character Martin Dee – himself something of a curiosity. He crops up as an extra in all manner of feature films and television dramas, and years ago, was occasionally featured on *That's Life*, playing 'tunes' on a bizarre array of implements! I've known Martin for many years, and recall with a tinge of sadness how, back in the 1980s, I attended his farm in response to the reported theft of a Charollais calf. There were no witnesses, of course, but crushed vegetation indicated where a large vehicle had backed up to a gate to load the animal. And there, too, up against the gate, was the calf's mother – desperately lowing over and over again, as though begging the return of her stolen calf. The sight and sound of that poor old cow upset me, and I wish I could have found her offspring.

Back down the hill, then, and through the village on the road towards Paxford, one comes to Northwick House. This mansion dates in part from 1686, though there were additions in the eighteenth and nineteenth centuries, and the building has now been converted into luxury apartments. It is an imposing house, visible from miles around. Easily unnoticed, however, is an ice house and a fountain set in grounds near the larger of two lakes. The fountain is thought to have been a gift from Lord Nelson to a former owner of Northwick Park, but is now almost completely overgrown. The ice house dates probably from the late eighteenth century or early nineteenth century. Before the use of mechanical refrigeration, ice houses were used in large houses for the storage of ice needed to keep food fresh, becoming quite common in the late seventeenth century. The ice houses, as in the one at Northwick Park, were built underground, with the entrance opening onto a passage leading to the chamber. As with many of the curiosities I describe, however, the ice house and fountain are on private land.

It is a short distance from Northwick Park to the neighbouring business centre, where various business enterprises occupy dour buildings constructed of red brick. The buildings were actually erected in the second half of the Second World War as an American army hospital, then after 1945, alterations were made to provide accommodation for Polish refugees, the area soon becoming known as 'The Polish Camp'. The Poles were to remain in residence there for more than twenty years, the last of the families being locally re-housed by 1970. During their occupation of the camp, it became virtually a 'Poland beyond Poland' and a significant feature of the site was a religious Marian shrine, built by the Poles in 1953, which stood on a stone plinth in a small enclosure at the edge of the accommodation buildings. When the camp was vacated the shrine was removed, but the enclosure and plinth remain as a curious feature of the business park.

A short drive through lovely scenery takes one via Draycott to the village of Aston Magna. Through the village, and on the eastern fringe, is the church, built in 1846 for Lord Redesdale. Redundant since the late 1970s, it is now a private dwelling, though a number of headstones are still visible in the churchyard. Though the church is perhaps not a building of architectural beauty, it is nevertheless an interesting curiosity.

South of the church are some roughly circular earthworks whose origin is something of a mystery. Usually described as the remains of a moat that surrounded a long-gone 'castle' or homestead, other opinion suggests the site to be the remains of a Neolithic henge of between 3000 and 4000 BC. Aston Magna's former name of Hanging Aston may, it has been suggested, originally have been Hengen Aston. To my mind the 'henge' theory seems a bit fanciful, and until proper archaeological examination takes place the origin of the earthworks remains open to conjecture.

Returning to the church, if one follows the lane to the left of the building's entrance, the old part of the village is found, with a small green in front of a farm and some pretty houses. On the grass verge are the base block and part of the shaft of the medieval village cross. Moss-covered and close to a hedge, these remains are easily missed. For me, this is the best part of the village – quiet, secluded and unspoilt.

In a dwelling house close by Aston Magna's redundant church are the remains of a chapel founded in Norman times, though its status as a place of worship was short-lived. It was stripped of its financial support by King Edward VI's Chantries

*The Polish shrine.*

Act of 1547 and had become a cottage by the early seventeenth century. The building retains the air of a church, however, and inside a significant portion of the Norman chancel arch, with one of its capitals, still exists. This is a private dwelling, however, and not open to the public. Leaving the village green, one passes a development of modern houses and crosses the railway bridge. I have been told that the curve in the line, visible as one looks north-west from the bridge, is the most acute on the old Great Western Railway line.

I think Aston Magna has a quiet and relaxed feel to it, and though one rarely reads anything particularly flattering about it, I have always found it interesting and appealing. There are pleasant views across to the valley of the Stour, with the trees of 'Brailes Clump' standing prominently on a hill to the east. Sadly, there is no post office, shop or pub. Luckily for me, I had my own source of refreshment. In the 1990s I was friendly with the local Neighbourhood Watch co-ordinator and he would often see to it that I received some liquid sustenance. But times change. He's moved to the Isle of Wight and I've left the Police…

Now, we've already seen lovely gardens at Sezincote, Bourton-on-the-Hill, Hidcote and Blockley, but the next village possesses the *pièce de résistance*. Batsford is about a mile south, on the road to Moreton-in-Marsh, but the real attraction of the village has to be approached from the A44 road between Moreton and Bourton-on-the-Hill. The village consists mainly of a little group of houses gathered near the entrance to Batsford Park – a neo-Tudor mansion designed by Sir Ernest George and built between 1888 and 1892 under the supervision of the architect Guy Dawber (later responsible for other significant architectural designs in the Cotswolds). The house was for a time the home of the famed Mitford girls when their father, Lord Redesdale, was resident. I happily recall how, years ago, I spent several enjoyable evenings in a flat on the top floor of the house. I was at the time friendly with a lady who lived in the flat, and she was kind enough to entertain me there on a number of occasions. I think that, as much as anything, the attraction was a mutual appreciation of red wine.

More interesting to many than the house itself, though, is the fine arboretum surrounding it, laid out by the 1st Baron Redesdale in 1888 as a 'wild garden'. This great collection of colourful trees from around the world is in a particularly attractive setting, looking down from a limestone ridge of about 800 feet above sea level across the Vale of Evenlode, towards Stow-on-the-Wold. Apart from the great number of species of botanical interest there are several curiosities to attract the eye. On the slope above the mansion there is a Chinese lion, a pair of bronze Japanese deer, and a bronze Buddha in the attitude of exaltation. Lord Redesdale brought all these from the Far East in the last quarter of the nineteenth century. Nearby is a Japanese rest house, while a short walk takes one to a statue of Daphne, sculpted by Simon Verity. According to Greek legend, the Gods turned her into a tree as she fled from Apollo.

Close to the arboretum there is a well stocked garden centre, which has an additional attraction in the form of 'The Apple Store', a delightful place to enjoy a snack and beverage. Nearby, too, there is a falconry, from where various birds of prey may be seen at close quarters. Indeed, a visit to the arboretum, garden centre and falconry can easily occupy an entire day.

Above Batsford Park, in fields off the unclassified road to Bourton-on-the-Hill and Blockley (an area known as Worcester Approach), there are reminders of wartime activity. Before embarkation to France for D-Day, substantial numbers of American troops with tanks were billeted in the North Cotswolds. The tanks would arrive, dismantled, in crates and would be assembled on site, and local people recall them being parked along the roadside at Worcester Approach. A local farmer, David Minett, remembers a platform being erected in a field, upon which General Patton addressed the assembled troops. Many of the soldiers were housed in huts in the fields and there still exists the concrete base upon which the cookhouse stood.

Completely unrelated, but interesting nevertheless, is a small memorial stone on the roadside verge of the lane between Moreton-in-Marsh and Batsford. Situated almost opposite Boreham Lodge, the stone, which has a little bowl sometimes filled with flowers until recent years, bears the simple inscription 'Martyn, Peter, John' and the date '12.9.71'. Some passers-by will no doubt have wondered about its origin. The stone marks the spot where a tragic road accident occurred one Sunday afternoon in September of 1971. Three young men were travelling towards Moreton-in-Marsh when the car they were occupying left the road and hit a tree, instantly killing all three. For many years the scarred tree could be seen as a grim reminder on the roadside, but it was cut down in the last decade of the twentieth century.

We now leave the northern-most tip of the Cotswolds and travel the six miles south to Upper Swell, following the A44 to Moreton, then the A429 to Stow-on-the-Wold, followed by the B4077 to Upper Swell. On the way down to the village, one passes Abbotswood, another beautiful garden open to the public on occasional Sundays. The village has a fine manor house and a pleasant little church, with a Norman south doorway within its fifteenth-century porch. There is a lane that runs alongside part of the pretty River Dikler towards Donnington Brewery, but probably the prettiest part of the village is set in the most potentially dangerous section.

Set in an idyllic Cotswold scene, the early nineteenth century mill, with its wheel still in operation, has a row of eighteenth-century cottages next to it. Next to these pretty buildings is a weir and mill pond – fed by the River Dikler, which runs beneath a three-arch eighteenth century bridge. The bridge is on a sharp bend, and the road is wide enough to permit the passage of only one vehicle at a time, so it is unsurprising that a number of road accidents – some very serious – have occurred here, damaging the parapet of the bridge on several occasions. So, please be especially cautious when driving in this vicinity.

As you might expect, Lower Swell is not very far from Upper Swell. This pleasing village has the B4068 road to Cheltenham running through it, but this is no longer the main road to Cheltenham, so is not as busy as the Fosse Way, nearby at Stow-on-the-Wold. Midway through the village is The Golden Ball inn, a quiet little hostelry that serves local Donnington Ales.

On the road to Upper Swell is the village church, which is Norman in origin, and at the opposite end of the village is the entrance to the aforementioned Abbotswood, a fine early twentieth-century house with lovely gardens. Situated in the grounds of Abbotswood, Lady's Well lies on the east side of the drive, a short walk from the lodge at the drive entrance. Thought to have been a sacred spring, the water flows into a little well-house, with a stone roof supported by upright stone slabs. After passing into the dip-well, the water overflows into the River Dikler.

On the left side of the road leading up the hill from Lower Swell to Stow-on-the-Wold is a remarkable eighteenth-century cottage in the Hindu style. In the cellar of the cottage adjoining the Spa House is a well, now dry, the water of which was discovered in 1807 to be rich in mineral deposits. There were dreams in some quarters that Stow might become a spa town to rival Cheltenham and Bath, and a spa house in ashlar, with elaborate oriental decoration, was added to the cottage. The dreams of prosperity did not become reality, however, and by 1930 the well was no longer in use.

There is much evidence of ancient history, too, in Lower Swell. Some of the barrows of a Bronze Age cemetery can be seen in fields between the village and Guiting Power, concentrated on Cow Common. Ten round barrows and one long barrow (from the Neolithic period) are situated within a few hundred yards. Most of these barrows have been examined, with the discovery of skeletal remains as well as cremations. Unfortunately, ploughing has substantially reduced the size and visibility of a number of the round barrows, but significant remains do still exist.

The Whittlestone, the remnant of a Neolithic long barrow, has been placed on the roadside verge next to the village hall. Formed of local oolitic limestone, it is heavily scarred and pitted and measures about 5ft by 4½ft. It is undoubtedly part of a Neolithic long barrow, and O.G.S. Crawford in his 1925 book *Long Barrows Of The Cotswolds*, made reference to the stone having been at one time situated on a hill 200 yards north-west of the church. A farmer had found a 'perfect set of teeth' when ploughing by the stone. He replaced them in the soil, but a later occupier of the ground had the stone hauled out of the ground. It was rescued by the local vicar, however, and for many years it lay in the vicarage paddock. Eventually it was placed at its present location where it bears a plaque, which reads:

THE WHITTLESTONE.
THIS ANCIENT STONE ORIGINALLY SITED ABOUT 200 YARDS
FROM THE NORTH WEST CORNER OF THE CHURCH IS
A RELIC OF THE NEOLITHIC AGE, C. 2000 BC, ASSOCIATED
PRESUMABLY WITH THE MODE OF HUMAN BURIAL
PRACTISED AT THAT PERIOD.

Finally, there is the Hoar Stone. This ancient megalith measures 3ft in height by almost 6ft in length and is to be seen in the middle of a field about half a mile south-west of the church at Lower Swell, a couple of hundred yards off the road to Upper Slaughter. In the evening light it can easily be seen standing alone in the pasture, the pale stone

*The Hoar Stone.*

shining in the fading sunlight. A local oolite stone, there is no trace of any tumulus or burial chamber stones, so it seems probable that it was placed in isolation.

From the B4068 at Lower Swell there is a lane leading south-west that runs directly to Upper Slaughter. Situated on the banks of the River Eye, Upper Slaughter is a pretty village with neat cottages, a shallow ford and a fine Elizabethan manor house.

Near the church are the remains of a motte and bailey castle, close to a bend in the river – here no more than a brook. The brook runs to the north of the substantial mound, while a moat was created on the east. Arthur Mee in his *King's England: Gloucestershire* describes the mound as having '…a flat top and the remains of a stone-lined well at the centre.' It is thought that the castle was used for a short period only, having been built purely for local defence. The precise date of the castle is uncertain but pottery from the eleventh to the thirteenth centuries has been found on the site.

Upper Slaughter residents received enemy attention during the Second World War. Hundreds of incendiaries fell around the village at a quarter to six on the morning of 4 February 1944, causing numerous fires and damaging buildings. Thankfully, no one was hurt and a plaque in the village hall commends the fortitude of the villagers. It seems the village was always lucky in war – as many as forty-four men went to fight in the First World War without loss, and in 1920 the village hall was opened to commemorate their safe return. Such villages – of which there are less than thirty in England – have become known as 'thankful villages'.

*Milton's Well at Upper Slaughter.*

A curiosity of far more peaceful origins can be seen near the banks of the River Eye, just inside the grounds of Eyford Park, where one can see a well that was built in 1975. Close by, however, is a much older well. Known as 'Milton's Well', it is made of stone, is of hexagonal design, and is about 2ft deep, with a small flight of moss-covered, worn stone steps leading down the banks of the river. Another flight of steps once led to a summerhouse. Just above the well is a stone wall, upon which is a brass plaque with the inscription:

MILTON'S WELL

TIS SAID BESIDE THESE LOVELY GLADES,
THESE CRYSTAL STREAMS, THESE SYLVAN SHADES,
WHERE FEATHERED SONGSTERS ON THEIR WING
IN HEAVENLY CHORUS JOIN AND SING.

THAT MILTON PENNED IMMORTAL LAYS
ON PARADISE AND HEAVEN'S PRAISE
EACH SUBJECT THERE THAT GREETS THE EYE
RAISES THE POET'S THOUGHTS ON HIGH

NO EARTHLY THINGS CAN THERE INTRUDE
ON LOVELY EYFORD'S SOLITUDE.
BUT BEAUTEOUS NATURE REIGNS SUPREME
AND PARADISE IS ALL HIS THEME.
W.H.C. PLOWDEN

THE ABOVE LINES WERE WRITTEN BY A FRIEND FOR
MRS SOMERSET D'ARCY IRVINE WHO RESTORED AND
EMBELLISHED THIS ANCIENT WELL IN THE YEAR 1866.

BESIDE THIS SPRING MILTON WROTE PARADISE LOST.

For many years the well was in semi-ruinous condition, but has recently been lov-ingly restored. It may be approached by crossing a stile and wooden bridge that passes over the river close to the drive to Eyford Park. The well is in a beautiful location, but is on private property and permission should be obtained before visiting it.`

The famous Lower Slaughter is just half a mile to the south-east. This delightful village is hugely popular with tourists and, because of this, it is probably better to visit out of season. The River Eye flows through the village, and can be crossed by a series of small bridges. The mill, with its tall chimney and mellow brick, is especially attractive – and much photographed.

Lovely though the old cottages are, it is worth mentioning a terrace of six mod-ern houses built in connection with the 1951 Festival of Britain. Standing at the northern edge of the village, close to the lane leading to Stow-on-the-Wold, these provide a good example of how a building need not be particularly old to blend into the Cotswold scene.

Though we are now less than a couple of miles from Bourton-on-the-Water to the south, the next stage of the journey involves travelling three miles to the west, to Naunton. Nestling in the valley of the River Windrush, Naunton is a truly lovely village. Most of its cottages and houses are pretty, and the church possesses a beautifully carved stone pulpit of about 1400. Of special interest, however, is the stone dovecote standing near the banks of the river. Built about 1600, and restored in 1949, it is thought that the roof may still contain some of its original timbers. When built, it would have been owned by a wealthy village resident, who regularly dined on the pigeons collected from their holes, though the identity of that origi-nal owner has long been lost in the mists of time.

In 1997 controversial plans to turn the dovecote into a house with bed-and-breakfast accommodation prompted villagers to raise funds to buy and restore the

*The Dovecote at Naunton.*

building. The dovecote is one of the largest in Gloucestershire, and, in its beautiful and tranquil setting, is well worth seeing.

A very pleasant walk can be taken by public right of way along the valley of the Windrush from Naunton to Bourton-on-the-Water. This takes one close to the ford near the site of the medieval village of Lower Harford. This is a picturesque spot, but be warned, the ford can be quite deep after wet weather.

By travelling for three miles to the south, along a narrow lane that passes Aylworth Farm (close to the site of the medieval village of Aylworth), one arrives at the village of Cold Aston. This high and exposed village has a little green with a sycamore tree growing upon it, a small Norman church and a pleasant pub, The Plough. Particularly lovely, however, is a lane that runs through open farmland and countryside, from Cold Aston to the village of Turkdean, a couple of miles south-west. Called 'Bangup Lane', it is no longer kept up by the Highways Authority and there is a sign that warns potential explorers that it is 'unsuitable for motor vehicles'. Certainly the ride can be a little rough, and exploration after a lengthy wet spell is not advised, but the lane's apparent inaccessibility is its main attraction. When trundling along its rough surface, windswept fields and bleating lambs all around, there is a definite sense of being in the 'real' Cotswolds.

It is also possible to get to Turkdean on a rather more serviceable road than Bangup Lane. From Cold Aston, take the lane east to Notgrove, then head south to Turkdean. This small hillside village has a Norman church with a fifteenth-cen-

*The Beech Avenue between Turkdean and Lower Dean.*

*The tunnel beneath the railway embankment at Salperton.*

tury pulpit, and a couple of very old farms – Rectory Farm, with a fourteenth- or fifteenth-century crypt, and Manor Farm of the sixteenth or seventeenth century.

Most impressive, however, is the hill down from the village to the neighbouring hamlet of Lower Dean. A steep bank of mature beech trees that forms an avenue either side of the road renders this especially captivating. Several hollows set into the bank are perhaps the remnants of very old quarries. Close to the foot of this hill is a lane that leads to Lower Dean, then on towards the A40. Just before the A40 is reached, a turn to the right takes one to Hazleton. From Hazleton a lane leads to Salperton, about five miles from Turkdean. A tiny village just off the A436 road between Cheltenham and Stow-on-the-Wold, Salperton has two features of interest to the curiosity-seeker. As one approaches from the A436 one finds the village nestling in a dip. If the sharp curve to the right is followed, slumbering cottages are passed until a high railway embankment is reached, much overgrown with trees and briars. Beneath the now redundant railway line is a high road tunnel, sturdily constructed of large blocks of local stone. The road seems to lead nowhere other than to a couple of private residences, but the quiet splendour of the tall embankment and tunnel are particularly impressive. The line originally formed part of the Banbury and Cheltenham Direct Railway, this section between Cheltenham and Bourton-on-the-Water having been opened in 1881. It closed in 1962, however, and now as one stands and stares in awe at this huge man-made earthwork, one hears not the whistle of an approaching steam engine but the drone of insects and the warble of small birds as Nature reclaims the land.

On the western side of the village a rather unusual war memorial stands in a small walled and paved enclosure, surrounded by fields. A tall wooden cross in representation of the Crucifixion is mounted on a square Cotswold stone block, inscribed with the names of those who died in the First and Second World Wars. It is an impressive memorial to the twenty-two officers and men who lost their lives. Erected in 1919, the memorial and courtyard are well tended, the gates at the entrance bearing the moving inscription 'Greater love than this no man hath that a man lay down his life for his friends'.

If the lane from Salperton to the B4068 is now taken, it will be found that it crosses the main road, before continuing on to the hamlet of Brockhampton a little over three miles away. A pretty place, with curious little lanes and paths, it has a very good pub The Craven Arms, tucked away along a narrow road.

Just over a mile north, on the way to Winchcombe, is peaceful Charlton Abbots. This small hamlet, where the monks of Winchcombe Abbey had a hospice for lepers, has delightful views over the Sudeley Valley from the churchyard. A fir plantation now stands on the site of the leper colony and nearby is a large moss-covered stone sheep

*The sheep wash at Charlton Abbots. (Photograph courtesy of J. Bolan.)*

wash, fed by a spring. This is reached by following an earthen path that branches off the gravel path running downhill to the church. The small Church of St Martin was ruinous in the eighteenth century, so was almost completely rebuilt, though some of the original thirteenth-century features have been incorporated into portions of the south doorway. The tub-shaped bowl of the font is thirteenth-century.

From a much earlier period is the barrow at Belas Knap. This well preserved, Neolithic, chambered long barrow, built around 3000 BC, is approached by walking for about three-quarters of a mile along a steeply wooded track, leading off Corndean Lane, about two miles from Winchcombe. Measuring 174ft long by 60ft wide, the barrow has a blind entrance at its centre and four burial chambers, which open from the long sides of the mound. Extensive excavations revealed at least thirty-eight skeletons, several of the skulls apparently having been dealt a heavy blow just before, or shortly after, death. The monument was sympathetically restored in the 1930s so that Belas Knap long barrow gives one a real idea of how these tombs must have looked five thousand years ago. Its high and windswept setting is particularly atmospheric, the enormous stones and whale-shaped mound adding to the sense of wonder.

When Corndean Lane arrives at Winchcombe, the temptation may well be to begin exploring this fascinating town. That can be done, of course, but the suggested course is to turn left along the A46 instead, and begin the climb to the top of Cleeve Hill. This imposing hill overlooking Cheltenham consists of common land, and slopes up to the highest point in the Cotswolds (1082ft). It is actually the largest uncultivated part of the wolds. The walking to be had on the hill is gentle and there are marvellous views over the Severn Valley, and beyond to the Malvern Hills and the distant mountains of Wales. Cleeve Hill may be approached from various places, including Corndean Lane – already described – and Postlip, both near Winchcombe, or from a number of clearly visible points adjacent to the A46 road at Cleeve Hill village, where there is roadside parking and public toilets.

Having enjoyed the fine views over Cheltenham, now turn right off the hill towards Woodmancote. This continues on to Gotherington, then to Prescott. A visit to this small hamlet is included chiefly because – as the home of the Prescott Speed Hill Climb – it is likely to be of considerable interest to motor racing enthusiasts. A number of championship meetings take place each year, where drivers in extremely powerful cars race against the clock over Prescott's course, which is a tough and steep road running up Prescott Hill. The event may well appeal to anyone curious about the sight of cars with ex-Grand Prix V8 engines roaring up the steep gradient of a Cotswold Hill. Information about events is obtainable from the Bugatti Owners' Club at Prescott Hill.

Gretton, the next 'stop', is a short drive east along a winding lane. A neat village that has half-timbered properties as well as Cotswold stone cottages, Gretton has a Victorian church, which was built to replace an earlier church building taken down at the turn of the nineteenth century. A fifteenth-century stone tower, with a pyramid-shaped roof topped by a weather vane, and known as St Philip's Tower, is all that remains of the demolished medieval church. The tower stands in a small, lawned enclosure, up a shingle drive leading between two delightful thatched cottages, about 50 yards from Working Lane. The Bugatti, in the centre of the village, is a good hostelry and acknowledges the nearby Prescott Hill Climb with its name. Another fine inn, full of character and charm, stands at the edge of the village. The Royal Oak has a very good beer garden and pleasant views towards Toddington.

It takes only a few minutes to drive to the next village, Greet, which is just outside Winchcombe. This hamlet consists mainly of modern houses, with little to attract the curiosity-seeker. There is a good pub, The Harvest Home, however, as well as the 'Winchcombe' stop on the Gloucestershire Warwickshire Railway line from Toddington. Here, at Winchcombe Station, a bit of 'Welsh-Cotswolds' can be seen. Well, it is Winchcombe Station now, right enough, but I remember it as Troy Station in my home town of Monmouth. The station was originally built by the Coleford, Monmouth, Usk and Pontypool Railway in 1857, but the passenger service closed in 1959, with freight usage ending in 1964. For years the old Troy

*The Former Monmouth (Troy) Station.*

Station stood more or less idly on the edge of Monmouth town, but was carefully taken down in the 1980s and rebuilt at Winchcombe. Looking at it now, it is hard to imagine it ever having been anywhere else. At the time of writing, there is talk of undertaking a similar – if rather less distant – move of the old station at Bourton-on-the-Water to Broadway.

Now travel south along the A46 for a couple of minutes and, at last, we arrive at Winchcombe. This is a lovely town, unspoilt and full of interest. Until the eleventh century, when it was taken into Gloucestershire, it was a Mercian capital. An abbey was founded here in 798 by the Mercian King Kenulf. According to legend, Kenulf's son, St Kenelm, was murdered, the abbey subsequently being dedicated to him. Pilgrims would then visit in their hundreds, all of this helping ensure the town's prosperity. Today, however, it is accepted that the tale of the murdered prince is wholly invention. In the thirteenth century a Benedictine abbey was founded here, to the east of today's church, and further prosperity followed.

Winchcombe's High Street is lined with lovely houses – some of stone, some half- timbered. The church is a marvellous building with many interesting features. A Perpendicular 'wool church' of the fifteenth century, the Parish Church of St Peter was built on the site of an earlier church, mainly due to the financial support of the abbot, William, and Lord Ralph Boteler of nearby Sudeley. The church has an imposing embattled tower with eight pinnacles, and the exterior is famous for its fascinating collection of gargoyles.

Bullets fired by Roundhead troops as they shot Royalist soldiers during the Civil War made the marks that can be seen on the external wall of the north aisle, at the west end. Inside the building, too, there is much of interest. At either side of the west end of the nave are stone coffins found during excavations on the site of the abbey in 1815. These are said to have contained the bodies of King Kenulf and his son, St Kenelm. Remnants of the abbey, in the shape of an oak door and floor tiles, can be seen in the north aisle. Close by is a sixteenth-century alms box. At the west end of the nave is a medieval oak screen, beautifully carved with lizards, vines, grapes and roses … and one mischievous face, known as the Winchcombe Imp. A former altar cloth can be seen in a cabinet near the north door, traditionally attributed to Catherine of Aragon, from when she stayed at Sudeley.

A short walk to the south of the town leads to Sudeley Castle, an impressive fifteenth-century building standing on the site of an earlier castle. The building was the home of Sir Thomas Boteler, Admiral of the Fleet, until it became Royal property after the War of the Roses. On the death of King Henry VIII in 1547, Queen Catherine Parr came to live at Sudeley. She died in 1548 and her restored tomb – desecrated in the Civil War – can be seen in St Mary's Chapel. After the Civil War the castle was substantially damaged by the Parliamentarians and became ruinous. By the middle of the nineteenth century, however, it had been much restored by John and William Dent – two brothers of Worcester, who purchased the estate – and has remained in the same family ever since. Sudeley Castle is full of interest and certainly merits a visit.

A couple of miles to the south-east of Winchcombe, deep in the heart of the Sudeley Valley, is an ancient monument that, to my mind at least, is among the most evocative in the Cotswolds. In the middle of Spoonley Wood, with a stream running close by, are the remains of a Roman villa, believed to date from the third century. It was quite a substantial villa, with a courtyard some 50 yards square, a mosaic-paved bathing area, and a wing which served as slave quarters – or, possibly, accommodation for another branch of the family. The ruins, which had been visible in the wood before 1877, were excavated in 1882. The walls were partly rebuilt on the east and south and a mosaic pavement was reconstructed in the bath area. These rooms were covered by wooden sheds but the shelters had collapsed by the 1960s and had completely disappeared by the late 1970s. A path and steps connecting the bathing area to the kitchen area remain discernible, however, and a well and remains of the central heating furnace are visible. Perhaps most excitingly, a good-sized section of the 'reconstructed' mosaic can be seen in what was the bathing area. A number of

*The Roman villa in Spoonley Wood.*

finds from the excavation can be seen at Cirencester's Corinium Museum.

The villa site is hugely atmospheric. Ivy and creepers hang down from trees and are entwined around the walls and in summer one can only get to the place by battling through dense undergrowth. My first glimpse of the limestone walls, gleaming in the shadows as shafts of sunlight filtered through the trees, was, to me, awe-inspiring. With the drone of summer insects buzzing in my ears, and mewing buzzards circling high overhead, I felt for a moment like one of the great explorers. Bill Bryson – that intrepid travel writer – seems to have been enthralled, too. In his 1995 book *Notes From A Small Island* he enthusiastically describes coming upon the remains. Fortunately there is a public footpath to the villa.

At Wadfield, just across the valley from the villa at Spoonley Wood, are the remains of another Roman villa. This was discovered in 1863 and was excavated in 1894-5, and today the remains are contained within a wooded enclosure. Part of a mosaic pavement has been reconstructed and is protected by a small building. This monument is on private property and is nowhere near as interesting or evocative – to the layman, at least – as its neighbour at Spoonley.

Standing in a commanding position on a hill about a mile east of Sudeley Castle is St Kenelm's Well. This is a charming little well-house over a spring, with a sculpture of St Kenelm above the doorway on the west side. The walls and roof are of local stone, with a well measuring 4½ft square, and 2ft deep, inside the building.

There is a seat in each corner. According to legend, Kenelm was murdered, after the death of his father, King Kenulf, at the behest of his wicked sister, Quenride, so she might reign in his stead. Following divine intervention, the monks of Winchcombe discovered Kenelm's body and were bearing it to the abbey, when they stopped to rest for the night. The well is supposed to mark the spot where the monks took rest. The original well-house was built, apparently, in the sixteenth century, but was embellished in 1887 by Emma Dent, of Sudeley Castle, to the pattern of a drawing dated 1572. On the north side a tablet bears the inscription:

OH, TRAVELLER, STAY THY WEARY FEET,
DRINK OF THIS WATER, PURE AND SWEET,
IT FLOWS FOR RICH AND POOR THE SAME,
THEN GO THY WAY, REMEMBERING STILL
THE WAYSIDE WELL BENEATH THE HILL,
THE CUP OF WATER IN HIS NAME.

Back in the centre of Winchcombe, one more curious place should be mentioned. In the back garden of a house in the High Street is a charming Railway Museum. The whole place has a delightfully amateurish feel about it and it is like coming upon someone's private collection – which is what it really is, I suppose – that one has been fortunate enough to gain access to. There are old sections of track, signal boxes with working levers and bells, which all are encouraged to operate, and there is a fenced-off area containing hens and rabbits. This is a marvellous place, and I fondly remember bringing my two young sons here on a number of occasions. The 'boys' have grown older now and are more interested in football and computer games than signal boxes. But I still love Winchcombe's Railway Museum – never, myself, having outgrown a fascination with signal boxes and bits of railway memorabilia – and will continue to visit from time to time.

When going out of the town on the road to Toddington, one comes upon a rather dull-looking business park on the left. But it is not quite as dull as might be first thought. Goff's Brewery, which began in 1994, occupies Unit 9 within the park and is likely to be of interest to anyone who enjoys decent beer. The brewery produces a number of pleasant ales – including 'Jouster' and 'White Knight' – and can produce beer with personalized labels, if required.

If we now leave Winchcombe on the A46 north towards Broadway, a turn on the right, which leads to Hailes, will soon be found. It is probable that most people who visit Hailes come to see the ruins of the thirteenth-century Cistercian abbey. Interesting though that monument is, the village's twelfth-century church, with its fine chancel wall paintings, is well worth visiting too. The paintings date from the fourteenth century and depict a shield of arms, as well as animals and monsters. Additionally, paintings can be seen in the nave, with St Christopher on the north wall and lurcher dogs hunting a hare on the south. Together with the church's medieval stained glass and fifteenth-century screen, the paintings provide visitors with a very interesting building.

Hailes Abbey was founded in 1246 by Richard, Earl of Cornwall. A Cistercian house of monks was founded by Richard's father, King John, the place becoming a place of pilgrimage after Richard's son, Edmund, gave the monks a phial of blood, which the Pope had authenticated as Christ's. At the Dissolution of the Monasteries in 1539 the abbey was surrendered to the King's agents, his Commissioner, Thomas Cromwell, watching the destruction (according to legend) from Beckbury Camp at Farmcote.

All that is left to be seen today are sections of walls and parts of the cloisters. A small museum has many interesting items on display, and, in such a lovely and peaceful setting, the haunting ruins are well worthy of a visit.

To get to Stanway, the next village that one should not miss, we need to go back out onto the A46, turn right towards Broadway, then turn right again within a very short distance. This sleepy village lies at the bottom of the winding road that runs down the long hill from Ford, Temple Guiting and other villages on higher ground. The hill is itself very scenic, being heavily wooded and affording excellent views towards Winchcombe and beyond. The views are probably best appreciated if one leaves one's vehicle at a small lay-by near the summit and walks down the hill a short distance to where the panorama may be seen. Close to the crossroads near the foot of the hill is a fine war memorial. A bronze of St George and the Dragon, by Alexander Fisher, is mounted on a stone column and plinth designed by Sir Philip Stott, with lettering by Eric Gill. This is a most unusual and very striking memorial. In Stanway church, also, there is a small bronze by Alexander Fisher.

Travelling from the crossroads into the village one comes upon the magnificent gatehouse to the Jacobean manor house, Stanway House. Dated to about 1700, the gatehouse is of stone, with the entrance through a wide archway. Though often ascribed to Inigo Jones, it is now believed to be the work of Timothy Strong of Taynton. The house itself stands in lovely grounds beneath wooded parklands, and through the latter years of the 1990s, and the early years of the twenty-first century, much has been done to reinstate an eighteenth-century water garden. From a stone summer house called the Pyramid, a cascade (the longest in England) of water descends into an ornamental canal. Additionally, there is a single-jet fountain, which at 300ft is the highest fountain in Britain and the highest gravity fountain

*Stanway Viaduct.*

in the world. Stanway House is regularly opened to the public (see notice at the entrance).

Of interest to those who enjoy a tipple is a brewery situated fairly near the house, where the excellent 'Stanney Bitter' is brewed. This very palatable ale is available at a number of pubs in the Cotswolds area.

Leaving Stanway House, and taking the road towards Stanton, one passes the village cricket ground on the left. Here there is a curious wooden cricket pavilion with a thatched roof, and set upon staddle stones. This was presented to the village by the writer Sir James Barrie, best known for his children's story, *Peter Pan*. A cricket enthusiast, he had visited Stanway in 1921, having been taken there by his secretary, whose parents owned Stanway House.

From a little further along the road one sees the great structure of Stanway Viaduct on the old Great Western Railway line from Cheltenham to Stratford-upon-Avon. During the construction of the section from Broadway to Toddington the viaduct was built, with fifteen arches of a span of 36ft and height of 50ft. The viaduct was built of Staffordshire blue brick and has a total length of 630ft.

On Friday 13 November 1903, a remarkable accident occurred during the construction of the viaduct, with three arches out of the ten that had been completed falling in, a fourth collapsing the following day. Two men working on the removal of false supporting arches were killed immediately, two others dying soon afterwards. Other workers were seriously injured. Heavy rainfall was blamed for the disaster, though the presence of a heavy crane on top of one of the arches was

*The gatehouse ruin of the original Toddington Manor.*

considered to have hastened the accident. The line, which had opened in 1906, was finally closed in 1976 – though there had been no regular passenger service for many years. The Gloucestershire Warwickshire Railway Society was formed in the same year and today operates at Toddington, from where there are steam train rides to Winchcombe, and to Cheltenham Racecourse.

It takes only a couple of minutes to drive from Stanway to Toddington. This village is probably as well known today for its steam railway preservation society, the Gloucestershire Warwickshire Railway, as for anything else. But, valuable though that society's work is, there is more than that to Toddington. Actually, the houses on the A438 road near the roundabout junction with the A46 near the railway are in a part of the village known as New Town. The old part of Toddington lies to the north-west. The nineteenth-century church there, with its fine tower and spire, is imposing. Inside the building there is an impressive white marble tomb of Charles Hanbury-Tracy, 1st Lord Sudeley of Toddington, and his wife.

In a field next to the churchyard are the crumbling gatehouse ruins of the seventeenth-century Toddington Manor, replaced in the 1830s by the splendid Victorian Gothic mansion that exists today. All that is left of the original manor is the ornate archway of the gatehouse, standing alone in this field. The present Toddington Manor has been empty for two decades, but a 2005 report in *The Times* stated that it had just been bought by the artist, Damien Hirst, to be used as a museum to house his own work. I remember attending there on police duty late at night on more than one occasion in the 1980s when intruders had been disturbed in the grounds.

Once I was taken around the cellars and shown what seemed to be a labyrinth of rooms and passages. I particularly remember how impressive it all was, even by torchlight.

As we leave Toddington along the A438 towards Tewkesbury, it becomes perceptible that the Cotswolds are being left behind. Alderton is only just over two miles from Toddington, but the classic Cotswold village 'feel' is already becoming far less apparent. Alderton rarely receives mention in guides to the Cotswolds, probably because its character seems more 'Vale of Evesham' than 'Gloucestershire Cotswolds'. There are quite a lot of plain modern houses, but several timbered and old thatched cottages in the area around the churchyard are quaint and pretty. The village school is a welcome sight, too, and it is pleasing to find that Alderton supports a village shop. The mainly fourteenth-century church was over-restored in the nineteenth century, but has a lovely air of serenity and is clearly much cared for. The thirteenth-century font, carved out of a Norman capital, is worthy of note. Near the font is a fourteenth-century oak chest with decorative ironwork.

From Alderton we go back onto the A438 road and turn right to head for the junction with the A435 Evesham Road at Teddington. At first glance the main feature of this village seems to be a large roundabout, which forms the junction for roads leading to Tewkesbury, Cheltenham, Evesham and Stow-on-the-Wold, and close to the roundabout is a petrol station. The village itself, however, is a short drive along the road to Cheltenham and has a church that includes a fine Early English tower arch and west window brought from the ruins of Hailes Abbey.

The most curious features of Teddington, however, are near the aforementioned roundabout, which, unsurprisingly, is no thing of beauty. On a patch of green opposite the Teddington Hands public house, and with the petrol station as a background, is the 'Tibblestone', an ancient standing stone used at one time as the boundary of the old Gloucester hundred of Tibblestone. This holed, rounded pillar stands about 4ft in height and may actually be a defaced Roman milestone. Hidden for years, it was rediscovered in 1948 when excavations were being made for the foundations of the petrol station. Expert help was obtained and it was concluded that the stone must be the Tibblestone – the subject of local tradition and folk memory, and shown on ancient maps of the area. The stone was re-erected at the side of the road, having been visible near the crossroads in the late eighteenth century. The name, apparently, means 'Theobald's Stone' and commemorates an early local landowner.

About 50 yards closer to the roundabout, and on the opposite side of the road, stands the 'Teddington Hands' signpost. The post is just over 10ft in height and comprises five sections held together by iron cramps set in lead. On top of the column is a short stone cylinder into which six hands are set in lead-lined slots. The present 'hands' are made of sheet iron and on top of the shaft is a finial, which is made of local limestone. The following inscription appears on the stone:

EDMOND ATTWOOD OF THE VINE TREE
AT THE FIRST TIME ERECTED ME
AND FREELY HE DID THIS BESTOW
STRANGE TRAVELLERS THE WAY TO SHEW
TEN GENERATIONS PAST AND GONE
REPAIRED BY ALICE ATTWOOD
OF TEDDINGTON. AUGUST 10TH 1876

The signpost points to six different directions: Overbury and Pershore; Evesham; Stow; Winchcombe; Cheltenham and Tewkesbury.

The next few villages are, frankly, barely within the Cotswolds. They are so close, however, that it seems sensible to include them, particularly as they are all of more than a little interest. Tredington, the next place to visit, is just over five miles south-west of Teddington. To find it, take the A435 road south from Teddington roundabout, turn right after a couple of miles until, just after it crosses over the M5 motorway, it reaches Tredington. This little village seems as much 'Vale of Evesham' as 'Cotswold', with a number of half-timbered houses. The small Norman church has an odd wooden tower, which was rebuilt in 1883, and in the churchyard are the steps and shaft of a fourteenth-century cross. Of most interest, though, is the south porch, for it contains the oldest object in the village.

Embedded in the limestone flagstones that pave the porch is a fossil ichthyosaurus – a 'fish-lizard' that lived in the early Jurassic age. To find a fossilized prehistoric creature in such a location is extremely unusual – perhaps even unique – and it can easily be seen if one lifts the mats that cover the floor. Do not expect to be faced with the imprint of some fearsome dragon, though. To the untrained eye, the fossil could be mistaken as no more than peculiar cracks in the stones.

Close to the River Severn, about two-and-a-half miles west of Tredington, is Deerhurst. With timber-framed cottages, and the River Severn flowing fairly nearby, Deerhurst appears somewhat removed from the Cotswolds. It is well worth visiting, however, as it possesses probably the finest example of a Saxon church in Gloucestershire, and one of the oldest churches in England. Deerhurst was first mentioned in AD 804, though the original church is thought to have been built in the 700s. The addition of a tower and chapels had taken place by the tenth century and today a number of notable architectural features from the ninth and tenth

*The 'Tibblestone' at Toddington.*

centuries remain, including a ninth-century font, which until its rescue in the nineteenth century had served as a horse trough.

A couple of hundred yards to the south-west of the church is a half-timbered farmhouse, with the small Anglo-Saxon Odda's Chapel at the west end. This Saxon building was a particularly significant architectural discovery of the nineteenth century. It was found in 1885 during repairs to the farmhouse, the sighting of a semi-circular arch leading to the discovery of a chancel and nave. An inscribed stone found in 1675 indicated that a royal hall – of which Odda's Chapel was a part – was dedicated on 12 April 1056. A number of features of Saxon architecture remain visible, including through-stones and 'long-and-short' quoins.

Tirley is about three miles west, and on the other side of the Severn. The village has a small fourteenth-century church, with a Norman font and a sixteenth-century alms chest, but it is Haw Bridge, which crosses the River Severn nearby, that has been of most interest to those with an interest in mysteries. As described earlier in connection with Leckhampton, it was here in January 1938 that bloodstained garments were found in the river near the bridge, then, a couple of weeks later, a man's headless and limbless torso was found by fishermen netting the river at Haw

*Ivor Gurney's Grave in Twigworth churchyard.*

Bridge. Meanwhile, a professional dancer named Brian Sullivan had been found dead at his home in Cheltenham, having committed suicide. This was at Tower Lodge, in the Leckhampton area of Cheltenham, as readers may recall. Additionally, one Captain William Butt had gone missing from his Cheltenham home and it became evident that he had been involved with Sullivan. Butt's bloodstained coat was found at Sullivan's home, and believing the headless torso to be that of Butt, police commenced a major search of the house and garden for the missing head.

The head never has been found, however, and no significant new evidence ever came to light. There the mystery remains: an unsolved 'murder of a person or persons unknown'. In 1958, some twenty years after the gruesome discovery, the bridge again made the news when it was badly damaged by a runaway barge. The present bridge was opened in 1961.

And now, to round off our exploration of the Cheltenham and North Cotswolds area, we drive east to join the A38 road towards Innsworth. After about six miles we arrive at the small and somewhat nondescript village of Twigworth. The place is noteworthy mainly as the last resting place of Ivor Gurney. A noted poet of the First World War, Gurney began his poetic career in 1917 and 1919 with two small books of poems titled *Severn and Somme* and *War's Embers*, though he has not always received recognition and fame comparable with some of his contemporary poets. He was born in Gloucester in 1890 and began to write music some fourteen years later, going on to win a scholarship to the Royal College of Music in 1911. Two years later he began to write verse and in 1916 fought in the trenches in France, where he suffered the effects of gassing. In the poem 'Portrait of a Coward' he wrote:

> True he'd have fought to death if the Germans came –
> But an hours battering after a days battering
> Brought his soul down to quivering, with small shame.

By 1918 he began to show signs of nervous breakdown and was subsequently discharged from the Army. In 1919 he returned to the Royal College of Music, being taught by Ralph Vaughan Williams. Meanwhile he continued writing poetry and had a number of poems published. By 1922, however, his mental health had deteriorated and he was certified insane. He continued to write poems and play music, but his condition worsened and he died on Boxing Day 1937. He is buried at Twigworth church.

# 2
# CIRENCESTER, STROUD AND THE SOUTH COTSWOLDS

Having covered many miles in Gloucestershire's North Cotswolds, and explored the area quite thoroughly, we will now move to the south of the district. To be perfectly honest, it would be almost impossible to say where the North Cotswolds area ends and the South Cotswolds area begins, but for the purposes of this book I am, in general, using the A40 road between Cheltenham and Burford as a convenient dividing line. In the North Cotswolds section we came down as far as Andoversford. From that village we now take the A436 road towards Gloucester, until just over its junction with the A435 (Cheltenham to Cirencester road) we arrive at Seven Springs, just outside the village of Coberley. At the roadside close to the junction stands a curious brick-built round house, with a conical thatched roof. Looking rather like an oversized pepper pot, it is actually a former parcel office, erected in 1840 by one William Hall, a local squire. The distance from Andoversford to Seven Springs is about four miles.

Along with Thames Head near Cirencester, Coberley is a claimant to the source of the River Thames. In a lay-by in a hollow beside the busy A436 road, and close to the round house building, is a spring – said to be the place where the Thames rises, though the accuracy of this claim is doubted. The water pours from holes in a stone wall a few yards from the road, to form a pool in an ornamental hollow surrounded by beech trees. As the name of this spot avers, there are actually seven springs rising at the location, one of which is definitely the source of the River Churn. Another is one of the many tributaries that make up the Thames, hence the claim.

Other than the seven springs and round house, there isn't very much to see here. There is a very large pub, The Seven Springs. Obviously geared primarily to dining, the place is more or less devoid of character. In fairness, though, satisfying meals are available at reasonable cost.

*The former parcel office at Coberley.*

The next place to look at is Crickley Hill Country Park. Another two miles or so along the A436 towards Gloucester, the entrance to the park is reached by going almost completely around a roundabout and following the B4070 towards Cheltenham. Within a matter of yards, the entrance will be seen on the left. A beautiful picnic spot, this imposing hill overlooking Gloucester, the Severn Valley and beyond, consists of over 100 acres of grassland and woodland, jointly owned by the Gloucestershire County Council and the National Trust. Open to the public as a country park, there are not only splendid views, but a dramatic rocky outcrop called the Devil's Table, readily visible from the parking area within the park, and the substantial remains of a settlement with Neolithic origins. Additionally, there are public lavatories and housed in a small building there is an exhibition detailing the park's history, wildlife and geology. In later occupation an Iron Age hillfort was constructed, and this has been the subject of detailed archaeological study. The fort is of major archaeological interest. By 2500 BC it was a fortified village - well protected by a deep ditch and a high rampart. When it came to an end is uncertain, but the end was certainly violent. Excavators found that the place was razed by fire, and many arrowheads were found. Fifth-century finds suggest that the fort might subsequently have been re-used in the Dark Ages.

Less than a mile south-west on the A417 road to Cirencester is another panoramic viewpoint, this time at Barrow Wake, near Birdlip. There is not a great deal to be seen at Birdlip itself, but the viewpoint gives a marvellous view out from the Cotswold edge and over the Severn Valley. On a clear day, one can see fine views of Gloucester, and beyond to the Malverns and the Welsh hills. The dramatic rocky face of Crickley hill can be seen to the north-west, crowned by its Iron Age hillfort. A stone indicator illustrates the geology of the area, and there are ample parking facilities.

From Barrow Wake we take the A417 towards Cirencester, then, after about two-and-a-half miles, a lane to Elkstone will be seen on the left. The village of Elkstone would be relatively uninteresting, were it not for the fact that one of the best preserved Norman churches in the Cotswolds is to be seen here. It has a fine Perpendicular west tower and a south doorway boasting splendid tympanum. The vaulted Norman chancel is full of architectural craftsmanship, and there are box pews and fine communion rails.

Return, now, to the A417 road and drive back in the direction of Birdlip for a short distance. Shortly, a lane on the left will be seen leading to Brimpsfield. There isn't a great deal to encourage the visitor to this little village near Birdlip, but it does have a history of some interest. Originally, the manor of Brimpsfield was given to the Giffard family by William the Conqueror, and a substantial stone castle, with a keep and four towers, was built in the thirteenth century (though a Norman castle made of wood was already situated on a mound near the Roman road, Ermin Street). They held it until 1322, when John Giffard was executed at Gloucester after he had joined the Berkeleys' unsuccessful rebellion against Edward II. The demolition of his castle was subsequently ordered, and five years later it was reported as 'dilapidated and fallen down'. Much of the stone from the ruin went on to be used in the building of houses in the village. Today the dry moat and south entrance survive and can be seen in the field on the right of the path approaching the church, and one is able to see the portcullis grooves in the lower stones of the gateway, as well as a few steps of the gatehouse stairs. The Church of St Michael is situated close to the castle earthworks. Parts of the building are Norman, though the tower rising from the centre of the building is fifteenth century. The churchyard has a number of table-tombs and in the south-west corner there is a Norman stone coffin lid with a large carved sword on it.

Just north of the church the few remains of the twelfth-century priory are to be seen built into the walls of a barn on the west side of the church, to the left of the churchyard. A trefoil and an arched window are discernible. The priory once belonged to the Benedictine monastery of Fontenelle in Burgundy – the church and a small grant of land were given to the abbot by a member of the Giffard family between 1086 and 1100.

*The view from Barrow Wake towards Crickley Hill.*

A lane running west from Brimpsfield to Cranham now needs to be followed for around two-and-a-half miles. Cranham is set in a deep hollow, surrounded by fine woodlands, mainly of beech. These consist of Buckholt Wood, Witcombe Wood, Brockworth Wood, Buckle Wood and Cranham Wood itself. All of these woods merit a visit.

The actual village of Cranham is unexceptional, though The Black Horse is a pub of character, offering a selection of ales and serving good food. Beyond Cranham Common the largely fifteenth-century Church of St James has an interesting curiosity in the form of two pairs of sheep-shears carved on the stone of the west face of the tower. It is thought these indicate that the building of the tower was paid for by a fifteenth-century wool stapler. Also of interest is a monument to Obadiah Done, 1738, which features cherubs holding wooden trumpets and palm leaves gilded with gold leaf.

The village has an annual feast and ox roast, which is held on the second Monday in August. This ancient tradition, revived in 1951, involves a procession and open air service, with venison for commoners and the Lord of the Manor.

Unfortunately, some of Cranham's most interesting curiosities are inaccessible. Cranham caves, which are actually old stone quarries from the nineteenth century, are situated beneath a section of the B4070 road. For many years the caves were left open and in the 1950s they were a regular meeting place for skiffle bands! In 1963 a boy got lost for some time in the caves and the entrances were subsequently sealed

*The 'poor souls' light' at the Church of
All Saints in Bisley.*

up for safety reasons. Nowadays they are home to bat colonies, and grills have been installed so that they are able to come and go unhindered. Disused stone quarries similar to those at Cranham exist at Minchinhampton and Whittington, but these, too, are inaccessible.

A drive of five miles has to be taken to get to Bisley, the next 'stop'. First, follow the lane leading east out of the village to join the B4070, then follow the road south – passing through a hamlet named The Camp – until Bisley is reached. A large village with some steep and narrow streets, and a number of fine houses and cottages, Bisley has several features of interest to the curiosity-hunter. The thirteenth-century Church of All Saints has a splendid spire, and though the interior was over-restored by the Victorians, there is an interesting effigy of a thirteenth-century knight and an elaborately carved font. Inside the Norman bowl are two fish carved in relief, apparently swimming in the water. Also of particular interest is the 'poor souls' light' in the churchyard, in which candles for the dead used once to be placed. The structure dates from the thirteenth century and was originally thought to be a well cover. It stands about 12ft high, six three-centred arches carrying a hexagonal pyramid. This unusual structure is thought to be the only one of its kind standing in a churchyard in England.

Near to The Bear Inn nearby is an interesting village lock-up, dated 1824, with an ogee gable and ball-finial. It has two cells – one for men, the other for women. It is believed that it was built to replace an earlier building, which stood next to the churchyard. A small plaque to the front of the building states it was 'a place of temporary confinement for wrongdoers awaiting appearance before the magistrate. In use until the 1850s. Restored 1999'. The Bear Inn was originally Bisley's Court House and Assembly Room, the building becoming an inn in 1766.

The inn building is particularly handsome, with a picturesque façade and over-hanging portico. In the bar there is a fine seventeenth century fireplace. Today the inn offers warm hospitality and serves excellent food and beers.

At the roadside just below the church, seven fountain heads in a row comprise Bisley Wells, where local people observe an ancient well-dressing ceremony each Ascension Day. This involves a procession of children carrying garlands of flowers, who gather at the wells for a service of blessing. The flowers are arranged to spell the word 'Ascension', the ceremony being followed by village sports, such as the sack race and the egg-and-spoon race. The fountain is in the form of a semi-circle, with the seven spouts at equal spacing. In 1863 it was restored by the Reverend Thomas Keble (brother of the founder of Keble College, Oxford).

Beyond Bisley village, on the main road to Stroud, are the remains of a cross dating from the eighth century, though only the base exists. It is a hexagonal structure, each side consisting of a three-centred arch. Its remote position suggests it must have been a preaching cross, while the letters 'BP' – for Bisley Parish – carved on the cross indicate that it has marked the parish boundary for a great many years. Apparently, it originally stood at the crossroads at Stancombe Ash, near Bisley, where it indicated the meeting place of the Bisley hundred.

When we get to Chalford, a couple of miles south, there is a fairly noticeable change of character. Built in terraces on the slopes of the Golden Valley, Chalford consists mainly of a haphazard jumble of cottages and houses, once the homes of weavers and clothiers, and has an almost Alpine appearance. Though attractive, the village is not particularly characteristic of the Cotswolds, and on the road to Stroud in the valley below, there are several former mills on the banks of the old Thames and Severn Canal. The growth of the village came about following the building of mills on the River Frome, and by the 1770s eight were working along the valley bottom. Most were cloth mills and by the early nineteenth century many struggled to survive, following depressions in the cloth industry.

Two old mill buildings worth seeking out are St Mary's Mill and Iles Mill, both fine buildings with interesting architectural features. St Mary's, which is reached by crossing the Gloucester-Swindon railway line, has a fine old iron water-wheel and is in an especially peaceful spot. The water-wheel is visible through easily accessible ground-floor windows. In order to cross the railway line, one has to ring a bell at the gate that blocks the lane, and a crossing-keeper will emerge from his hut to allow access. A heavily be-whiskered railwayman opened the gate when I visited, reminding me of a character one might have seen in the film *Oh, Mr Porter!*

Iles Mill, nowadays a private dwelling, uses power created by a water turbine. Crystal-clear, the River Frome runs alongside the mill, and when I visited, a handsome ginger cat named Cuthbert could be seen sitting at one of the windows. His owners showed me hospitality and kindness, ensuring I would fondly remember the Chalford mills. Facing the church is the Round House, which was built in 1790 as a watchtower for the Thames and Severn Canal. The canal, which closed in 1911, connected the River Severn with the Thames at Lechlade and the Round House would have housed a lengthman who was responsible for ensuring the boatmen observed the relevant bye-laws, and for maintaining the towpaths and fences in his section. The Round House has been sensitively restored as a private house.

Brimscombe is about a mile to the west of Chalford. It is clear to see how the Industrial Revolution affected the development of this village in the Golden Valley, with a number of industrial buildings visible near the old Stroudwater Canal. The Port Foundry stands on the site of the 'port' – a large sheet of water known as Brimscombe Basin – which was once the headquarters of the Thames and Severn Canal. Here the Severn trows used to bring coal, salt and slate from the River Severn and along the Stroudwater Canal for transhipment to the Thames and Severn Canal. The port has gone, filled in years ago, but at the western end The Ship Inn stands at the canalside. The inn sign depicts a sailing trow, indicating the importance of this once-busy canal transhipment point.

From Brimscombe we now follow the A419 alongside the River Frome for about a mile and a half until we arrive at Stroud. This town became industrialized in the eighteenth and nineteenth centuries, with well over 100 cloth mills in the five valleys that are centred on Stroud. The town became renowned as a centre for cloth, though competition from Yorkshire and abroad has rendered this flourishing industry more or less locally defunct. Two cloth companies continue, however, and various light industries have sprung up around the area. The town itself is not of great beauty, but there are a couple of interesting museums – the Industrial Museum and Stroud Museum.

The church is relatively uninteresting, but does have a fine fourteenth-century tower. In the churchyard, too, there is a curious 'above-ground' grave, described by John Timpson in his 1989 book *Timpson's Towns of England and Wales*. One John Hollings of Stroud was told in a disagreement that it was hoped he would be seen

*The Round House Chalford.*

'safe underground'. Though the adversary did indeed live longer than Hollings, his malignant hope was to remain unfulfilled. Hollings had left instructions that his coffin should not be buried, but be covered with a pile of stones. This is exactly what happened, and the grave, which does consist of stones – albeit neatly constructed, rather than merely 'piled' – can be seen in Stroud's churchyard.

Near Stroud's railway line, the first lock at the western end of the Thames and Severn Canal (1789-1911), by the junction with the Stroudwater Canal, was restored in the latter years of the twentieth century and makes an interesting feature. A pleasant walk can be obtained by following the towpath of the Thames and Severn Canal from its start to Daneway, where there is a welcoming pub, The Daneway Inn. I remember how in 1980, while I was a policeman stationed at Cheltenham, I found myself a little short of company, so joined the local 18 Plus Group. They were an interesting crowd and always seemed to be organizing some new outing or expedition. I recall that, on one particularly hot summer's day, we walked the length of the Thames and Severn Canal, and I remember being grateful of the shade provided by the many willow trees that grew alongside the old canal. We made it to The Daneway Inn, too, and much well-deserved ale was quaffed.

As a policeman I never had a great deal to do with Stroud. New recruits tended to get posted to Gloucester, Cheltenham or Stroud, and, as I've said elsewhere, I was

*A lock on the Thames and Severn Canal.*

posted to Cheltenham. Then, when I was moved to the North Cotswolds, I thought it fairly unlikely that I would ever be called upon to work at Stroud. Imagine my surprise and consternation, then, when on the Millennium New Year's Eve I found myself on patrol in Stroud. Perhaps 'patrol' isn't strictly accurate, though. By this time my MS symptoms had begun to manifest themselves and so I performed plain-clothes duty with a colleague in a CID vehicle. And as it turned out, the youth of Stroud were generally well-behaved, despite earlier fears of drunken over-exuberance. So much, then, for my experience of Stroud.

Now we must follow the B4070 road north-east for just over a mile to the village of Slad, where poet and author Laurie Lee spent his childhood – so brilliantly evoked in his book *Cider with Rosie*. Slad is small and unspoilt, and has an excellent inn, The Woolpack, where Laurie Lee was a regular. From the inn there are fine views over the Slad Valley, and for real ale enthusiasts the excellent beers brewed at nearby Uley are available.

Painswick is about a mile and a half to the north-east. The streets are narrow, and lined with many architecturally pleasing buildings, and there are numerous interesting shops and welcoming inns. Most visitors, though, will be attracted to Painswick's church and churchyard. The church has a fine steeple and a number of interesting monuments in its interior, but of particular note is the churchyard, where there is a very fine collection of table and pedestal tombs. Many are the work of John Bryan, who died in 1787 and is buried in a plain stone pyramid, thought to be based upon the tomb of Caius Cestius in Rome. Also notable are the clipped yews in the churchyard, most of which were planted around 1792. Each year on the Sunday following 19 September a traditional 'clipping' ceremony is held. This ceremony does not actually involve trimming the yews – *Clyppan* is an old Anglo Saxon term meaning 'to encircle' – and instead children with garlands, together with the clergy and choir, sing traditional hymns and hold hands to encircle the church. The ceremony is known to have been performed intermittently in the early nineteenth century, but was revived as an annual tradition in 1897.

The church was damaged during the Civil War, and impressions left by cannon balls can still be seen below the clockface on the tower. Also of interest is a pair of very unusual iron 'spectacle' stocks, thought to date from the seventeenth century, which can be seen against the churchyard wall near the gate to the south of the church.

A trek of about five miles, over hills and through woods, has to be taken to get to Haresfield, below Haresfield Hill to the west. It is a worthwhile 'trek', though, and takes one first through the pretty little village of Edge, before encountering several beautiful beech woods.

Haresfield itself is a pleasant enough village on the Cotswolds edge, with a number of old houses and a church with a fourteenth-century tower. Close to the church is an ancient mound called 'The Mount' and said to be of Danish or Saxon origin. Overgrown, and surrounded by a water-filled ditch, its purpose is obscure.

Close to the Gloucester-Bristol railway line, which cuts through the edge of the village, is a friendly inn, The Beacon. And when I say the railway line passes close, I mean *close*. One could easily imagine trains stopping to pick up passengers from the bar.

To the south-east of the village, the hilltop site of Haresfield Beacon, owned by the National Trust, affords panoramic views over the Severn Valley and Berkeley, and on to the Forest of Dean and South Wales. The hill is surrounded by the extensive earthworks of an Iron Age fort. The beacon itself is 713ft above sea level and there are ample car parking facilities for those wishing to explore, with a topograph situated close to the Shortwood car park. A short distance to the north, and close to the public road, is Cliff Well, where there is a small well house dated 1870, bearing the inscription:

Who'er the bucketful unwindeth
Let him bless God, who water findeth
Yet water here that shall availeth
Go seek that well that never faileth

*The Cromwell Siege Stone.*

Next to the well is a surfaced path leading into Cliff Wood. A few hundred yards along the path will be seen the Cromwell Siege Stone – a monument erected in the nineteenth century to commemorate the lifting of the Royalist siege of Gloucester on 5 September 1643, following the capture of Cheltenham by the Roundheads under the Earl of Essex. Though the Siege Stone is itself relatively unimpressive, there are fine views to be had from it – particularly in winter, before the trees are in leaf.

Frocester is getting on for seven miles to the south of Haresfield. From Haresfield village take the lane south to Little Haresfield and Standish, then continue to Stonehouse. Frocester will be found some two miles to the south-west of Stonehouse. This small village has a tithe barn at the Medieval Frocester Court, regarded as one of the finest in England. About a mile to the west of the village are the remains of what is known as the 'old church'. They consist of a lych gate and a Victorian Gothic tower and spire, all that remains of the village's original medieval church.

We now continue the 'tour' by travelling east from Frocester, on the Bath Road to Leonard Stanley, before negotiating the steep hills around Selsley Common. We then turn right and head south along Water Lane to Woodchester. An enjoyable diversion can be had by visiting Selsley Herb and Goat Farm in Water Lane, where there is a lovely herb garden – the goats being kept in an orchard!

*Remnants of the demolished Church of St Mary in Woodchester.*

Woodchester is a pleasant village with several eighteenth- and nineteenth-century mills in the valley bottom. The village's old Norman Church of St Mary was demolished about 1860 and replaced with a new building to the south of the village. Little remains of the old church, though there is a Norman chancel arch and north doorway, and there are some gravestones of interest. In the north-east corner of the old churchyard there is a tomb with a triangle to represent the Trinity inside a circle for Eternity. Also in the churchyard, buried beneath the soil, is the finest Roman mosaic in England, discovered in 1793. This used to be uncovered for public viewing every ten years, but this no longer takes place.

The village of Woodchester is probably best known for its unfinished mansion. In 1845 Woodchester Park estate and mansion, in a valley a few miles south of Stroud, was purchased by William Leigh from the Ducie family. Leigh wished to improve the mansion building, but on the advice of architect Augustus Pugin, demolished the house, then finding Pugin too expensive, commissioned local man Benjamin Bucknall to design a new house, and in 1854 building began on the site of the old building and terrace. The resulting mansion was substantial, in a Tudor, Cotswold style, Bucknall's design making full use of the expertise of French theorist Viollet-le-Duc. The skills of French masons were used, and wherever possible stone was used in preference to other materials.

Building work was well advanced by 1858. But then the money ran out, and in about 1870 work suddenly stopped. Though the bulk of the structural work had already been done, everything was left exactly as it stood – the builders downed tools and walked out, even leaving ladders propped against walls. Sections of the house were open to the roof, doors lead nowhere and upper corridors ended suddenly at ledges with the ground visible far below. Why the mansion was never finished has always been something of a mystery. The most plausible explanation is that Leigh had over-reached himself – as well as the mansion, he had funded the building of a monastery – and had found funds running low. Additionally, his health was failing and doctors advised him against living in the mansion, which is in a damp valley. He died in 1873 and the building was left to his son, who decided against spending money on it. Thus the mansion has remained a three-quarters finished building ever since. In 1987 Stroud District Council bought the house to save it from ruin, and two years later a trust was set up to raise money for repairs and adaptions.

Near the mansion is an excellent pub, The Ram Inn, where fine beer from the nearby brewery at Uley can be obtained, as well as several other real ales. Almost four miles to the west of Woodchester is Coaley Peak. From the peak, high above Frocester, there is a picnic area and viewpoint with fine views across the Severn Estuary, and beyond to the Forest of Dean and Wales. This is a very popular picnic area and is much frequented by walkers. The area is rich in wildlife and, when I visited, I enjoyed the sight of several buzzards circling in the sky overhead. The villages of Nympsfield and Uley are nearby, where Uley Bury hillfort and the long barrow called Hetty Pegler's Tump can be explored. A cosy and welcoming pub, The Fox and Hounds, is to be found in Coaley village itself – below the peak – and good food can be obtained, as well as ale brewed at the nearby Uley Brewery.

Uley is a very picturesque village a mile and a half south of Coaley Peak. A prosperous cloth centre before the Industrial Revolution, Uley has a number of pleasing eighteenth-century houses and an impressive Victorian church above the deep valley in which the village nestles. Next to the churchyard there is a path that leads up the hill to Uley Bury hillfort, one of the largest Iron Age forts in Gloucestershire. Probably constructed about 300 BC, it is roughly rectangular and occupies a promontory position. The fort has three lines of defences, with entrances at the south, east and north corners. A gold coin of the Dobunni tribe has been found here, and excavations in 1976 at the eastern entrance revealed a cobbled roadway leading into the fort. The interior of the fort has not been examined, but aerial photography has revealed numerous crop marks indicating the presence of internal compounds, boundary ditches and probable houses. A walk around the ramparts provides fine panoramic views over the Severn Vale.

Above: *Hetty Pegler's Tump.*

Left: *The grave with a bronze bee in the churchyard at Owlpen.*

To the north of the village is Hetty Pegler's Tump. A Neolithic long barrow, thought to date from about 2900 BC, it is situated about a mile north of Uley Church and is the one Cotswold barrow which offers the visitor a real impression of what these tombs must have really been like. Named after Hester Pegler, the seventeenth-century owner of the field, the grass-covered mound is 120ft long by 85ft wide at its east end, where a forecourt gives access to a gallery from which two pairs of side chambers lead off. Excavations in 1821 and 1854 revealed the presence of at least fifteen skeletons. The tomb has been restored and entry into the chamber can be gained by obtaining a key locally – information available at the monument.

In 1985 the Uley Brewery opened in the village. The fine ales that are produced there can be sampled at a number of pubs in the Cotswolds area, including a very hospitable free house, The Old Crown, situated near the brewery. I found 'Uley Bitter' to be an especially palatable ale, though some may prefer the stronger 'Pigs Ear' brew. The church and the pub are the main focal points of the village, but there is a useful village store and post office, too. When I visited the pub, I tripped and fell *before* having had a drink! The staff and patrons were very helpful, however, providing antiseptic cream and plasters for my grazes.

Owlpen, the next 'stop', is just half a mile east of Uley, along Fiery Lane. In a hollow in woodlands, the village forms a lovely group of buildings in a glorious setting. These include a very picturesque fifteenth-century manor house, an eighteenth-century mill and a pleasant Victorian church, its chancel elaborately decorated with inlaid mosaics. An alabaster cross on the altar is ornamented with twenty-nine amethysts. The church was rebuilt in 1828-30, a relic of the original building surviving in the form of the Norman bowl to the font. In the churchyard one grave has a curious headstone, designed by Bryant Fedden, which is decorated with a bronze bee.

There is not very much to see at the village of North Nibley. The church is quite attractive and has a nineteenth-century French-Gothic chancel of some note, having been designed by J.L. Pearson, who created Truro Cathedral. There are good views across to Stinchcombe Hill.

The nineteenth-century Tyndale Monument is the attraction for most visitors, however. The monument is reached by travelling the B4060 road from Gloucester, then a couple of hundred yards past The Black Horse Inn, following a pathway leading up the hill. The monument is in memory of William Tyndale, who, after ordination in 1521, became tutor to the sons of Sir John Walsh at Little Sodbury Manor in Gloucestershire. Tyndale subsequently moved to London and began translating the New Testament into English. Falling into conflict with the Church, he fled to Europe, in 1525 commencing printing his translations at Cologne. In

*The railway accident memorial at Churchend.*

1535, at the instigation of Henry VIII, he was arrested at Brussels and was executed the following year. The Tyndale Monument was built in 1866. Climbing the 121 steps to the monument's observation platform is rewarded with breathtaking views over the Severn Vale and beyond to the Forest of Dean.

For me, the feeling at this part of the journey was that I was now in almost foreign territory. It is a drive south-west of just over four miles, along Swinhay Lane and over the Gloucester–Bristol railway line, to the village of Charfield – the most southerly destination on this merry jaunt. Unfortunately, Charfield village will in some quarters always be associated with one terrible event. A dreadful railway accident occurred on the main line from Gloucester to Bristol at this little village near Wotton-under-Edge on 13 October 1928. Following driver or signalling error – it was never established beyond doubt where the blame lay – a collision involving three trains took place close to a bridge over the line. Escaping gas from the wooden coaches ignited almost immediately and the debris piled against the bridge rapidly became an inferno, which blazed for twelve hours. Fifteen lives were lost, including two children, whose bodies were unrecognizable. They were unconnected with any of the other victims and their identity was never established. No one ever came forward to claim them. It is a sad story, and even after all these years have passed by, it is difficult not to feel a tinge of sorrow for these two lost little people.

If one follows the road south out of Charfield to its hamlet of Churchend, one comes upon the old medieval parish church. The church is now redundant, but in a corner of the churchyard is a memorial cross of grey granite, which remembers the victims of the railway disaster. Those who lost their lives are named – but the unidentified children are listed as 'two unknown'. The question of who they were remains unanswered and the mystery has caused much speculation over the years, with various outlandish theories being suggested. Some believe the two were not children but jockeys and in 1937 a London woman claimed the bodies were those of her two young brothers. The claim, however, seems to have been dismissed.

From 1929 to the 1950s an elderly woman dressed in black was seen to visit the memorial two or three times a year. Arriving in a chauffeur-driven limousine, she would pray at the cross and leave flowers, but no one ever spoke to her and who she was is unknown. She has not been seen in the churchyard for almost half a century, and it is assumed that she died many years ago. With the passage of time it becomes ever more likely, of course, that the 'two unknown' will remain nameless.

And now we turn around and head north once more. It is almost two miles along the B4058 road to Wotton-under-Edge. This picturesque market town, with narrow streets and old houses, shelters below the fine beech trees of Westridge Wood. It was a prosperous wool centre in the seventeenth and eighteenth centuries, having been completely rebuilt after it was destroyed by fire in King John's reign, when the king's mercenaries are said to have torched the town as revenge upon the Berkeley estates.

Wotton has several curiosities. The Tolsey House, on the corner of High Street and Long Street, was formerly used for both borough court and prison. The cupola has an interesting copper weather vane, in the form of a flying dragon. Nearby, in Orchard Street, a house bears a plaque to show that one Isaac Pitman perfected the invention of shorthand there in 1837. Nearby, in a road called Potters Pond, is an ancient building that claims to be Wotton's oldest house. The thirteenth-century Ram Inn is a fine old building, with ancient timbers running through its walls, but, when I visited, looked to be in need of some renovation. A plaque on the wall reads: 'Here lodged the carpenters and stonemasons while building the parish church during the 13th century'. The Ram Inn, which is believed to have been built in 1145, ceased trading in 1967 and is nowadays home to spirits of a different kind. It is reputedly 'the most haunted house in

*The former Ram Inn in Wotton-under-Edge.*

Britain' and is regularly visited by sleuths and investigators, hoping to catch the ghostly entities on film. The owner of this former inn is happy to show visitors into the building, where the fascinating décor is in keeping with the great age of the place.

If one leaves Wotton-under-Edge by the B4058 road, which winds up the hill towards Nailsworth and Tetbury, one is confronted by a very impressive set of strip lynchets on the hillside ahead. I think these huge 'steps' in the ground are easily the most dramatic cultivation terraces in the Cotswolds. As at Temple Guiting, in the north of the area, these strip lynchets are likely to be Anglo-Saxon or medieval, and are the result of ploughing horizontally alongside the hill (rather than vertically against the gradient), which caused furrow slices to fall downhill, creating level terraces – the balks between them becoming steep banks. Over a period of time this build up of soil became quite pronounced, thus creating the striking 'lynchets' we see today.

Soon after passing through the tiny hamlet of Holywell, almost opposite the strip lynchets, take a turn right and follow the lane to the very small village of Ozleworth. This is about two miles from Wotton-under-Edge. Behind Ozleworth Park in the village is a small Norman church, standing in a circular churchyard. The church is particularly notable for its rare central hexagonal tower, dating from the twelfth century. There are a number of other Norman architectural features,

*The hexagonal church tower in the village of Oozehvorth.*

including an early thirteenth-century font. Ozleworth is really little more than a small group of buildings in a wooded valley, but it is worth visiting not only for its curious church tower, but for the quiet and unspoilt setting.

Leighterton is the next port of call. To get there, head north out of Ozleworth, and turn right along Ashcroft Road after a mile or so. This leads to a hamlet named Bagpath, and then to Scrubbett's Lane and Boxwell Road. We then cross the A46, by a little building that is appropriately named Cross Roads Lodge, to take the lane to Leighterton. There isn't much of interest at the village itself, but in a field on the right – about midway between the village and the A46 – there is a huge long barrow, known as West Barrow. A particularly large barrow, it measures 220ft long, and 20ft high at the east end. Now fairly substantially overgrown with trees, it was roughly excavated in 1700 with the discovery of 'three vaults arched over like ovens', each containing an earthen jar containing burnt human bones. The 'ovens' were probably burial chambers, but the workings were left open to the elements and no trace remains of the stones. The barrow dates from about 3500 to 2500 BC.

*Egypt Mill in Nailsworth.*

About four miles east of Leighterton, near the attractive town of Tetbury, is Highgrove House, the Gloucestershire home of HRH the Prince of Wales. As you might expect, a number of police officers are deployed there and, after speaking with various colleagues who performed duty at Highgrove, one hears a few yarns – some more believable than others. The impression that officers formed of 'the Royals' seemed favourable, and Princess Diana, apparently, was not above occasionally calling in at the police office to chat with the duty policemen. Personally, I didn't have occasion to visit Highgrove until, in 2002, I was privileged to be presented with a Police Long Service medal by Prince Charles.

However, if we now take the lane, known as Whitewater Road, north out of Leighterton the A46 will again be reached. The road follows a north-easterly direction until, after a mile, a road on the left leads to Newington Bagpath. This is a tiny place. A castle mound surrounded by a ditch, about 150ft in diameter, that runs into the fall of a steep scarp is all that remains of a medieval castle that stood here. Close to the earthworks is the small Church of St Bartholomew, originally Norman, but with its chancel rebuilt in 1858. Outside, from the churchyard, there are lovely views over a steep-sided valley.

About half a mile to the south of the church, and beside a public footpath, is a pillow mound – an artificial rabbit warren, where rabbits were used for their fur and as a meat source. The origins of this mound are obscure, but it may well have been connected with nearby Lasborough Manor.

Now returning to the A46, it is about four miles north to Nailsworth. This busy town has a number of interesting shops and welcoming pubs. The George Inn is particularly good, serving several fine ales and enjoying a reputation for excellent food. A sizeable stone clock tower on a green in the centre of Nailsworth was erected in 1951 in memory of those who fell in the two World Wars. Much of the town's individuality, however, is owed to the establishment of the cloth industry, and the many mills on the various brooks that join to form the Nailsworth stream.

Begun in the fifteenth century, the local cloth industry has left its mark with the numerous mill buildings that survive from the seventeenth, eighteenth and nineteenth centuries. Of particular interest are Egypt Mill, now a welcoming and unusual restaurant, and Dunkirk Mills, with striking architecture and now sympathetically converted to apartments. These mills are on the main road to Stroud, but on the old road to Bristol is another impressive mill, in an especially charming setting. Ruskin Mill, formerly known as Millbottom Mill, overlooks a large mill pool that is much frequented by ducks. Here, too, there is a pleasant coffee shop and an organic food store, as well as an interesting craft centre.

These old relics of the cloth industry are thoroughly interesting and greatly add to the charm of the area. The poet W.H. Davis must have liked the place, for he made Nailsworth his last home.

Amberley is just over a mile to the north of Nailsworth. Much of the well-known novel *John Halifax, Gentleman* was written there when its authoress, Mrs Craik, lived for some time at Rose Cottage. Not much else brings this scattered village to mind, though it was occupied by our ancient ancestors, with earthworks, burial mounds and barrows common hereabouts. Just outside the village, on Minchinhampton Common, is a long barrow that has been greatly disturbed – to a point where it is difficult to ascertain its precise dimensions. It is known as 'Whitefield's Tump', and is of interest, mainly because of a long-standing tradition that the Methodist evangelist George Whitefield (1714-1770) preached from its summit in 1743. Barrows have been used for all manner of purposes, but this is the only known case where one has been used as an ad-hoc pulpit. The image of a preacher holding forth from the summit of an ancient tomb on this desolate and windswept common is curious indeed.

Situated on the border between the Cotswolds and the Severn Vale, some four and a half miles south-east of Amberley, is the pleasant village of Avening. It was

*The Tingle Stone.*

once busy with the manufacture of cloth, at least two mills working on the stream that runs through the village. A footbridge consisting of one very large stone has been laid across this stream. Cloth is still made at Longford Mill, towards Nailsworth, but Avening is nowadays a fairly quiet place. Unlike so many Cotswold villages, it does have several shops and pubs – The Bell Inn in the High Street has a very good reputation.

Avening has a fine Norman church, too, which still has many of its original features. A few hundred yards north of the church, however, and set close together at the foot of a bank, are antiquities from a much earlier period of history. These are three stone burial chambers, which were erected in 1806, having been removed from a long barrow nearby – they are supposed to have the same relationship to each other as they originally had in the barrow. Two of the chambers have large cap-stones and the remnants of 'port-hole' type grave entrances. In her book *Prehistoric and Roman Monuments in England and Wales* Jacquetta Hawkes describes one of the entrances as 'among the best examples of a "port-hole" entrance in all Britain.'

Additionally, Avening has two long barrows of interest, both situated on the Gatcombe Park estate. Potential visitors to these monuments should be aware that they are on regularly patrolled Royal property, so access without permission is definitely not advised. The first of these barrows is the Tingle Stone long barrow. Surrounded by beech trees, this well-preserved barrow is 130ft long and 70ft wide. At the north end of the barrow, standing some 6ft high, is the 'Tingle Stone' – a large stone megalith thought by some to be the remains of a burial chamber. I, however, tend to share the view of historians who contend that there never was more than one stone on the barrow.

The second barrow is situated on a ridge just above Gatcombe Lodge, at the northern end of Gatcombe Park. It measures about 190ft long by 70ft wide, with a burial chamber on the north side, near the east end. This consists of five uprights with a capstone roof. In 1871 a skeleton was found here. Jacquetta Hawkes in *Prehistoric and Roman Monuments in England and Wales* describes this monument as 'an unusually fine long barrow', adding that the burial chamber's 'shadowy opening below a lintel stone has a romantic fairy-book air'. That book was published in 1951, however, so it will come as no surprise to find that the fairy-book air has substantially faded.

Minchinhampton, the next 'stop', is about three miles north-west of Avening. This little town has a splendid seventeenth-century Market House, supported on stone columns, and the church, which dates from the twelfth century, is interesting and attractive, possessing a fourteenth-century octagonal font, retrieved from the rectory garden in 1915. A mile north-west is Minchinhampton Common, almost 600 acres of turf country with excellent views and interesting archaeological remains dating from the Iron Age.

At the top of the common is a place where five roads meet, marked by a road sign named Tom Long's Post. Tom Long is supposed to be buried at this spot, having committed suicide, though there is another story that claims he was a highwayman. As at so many crossroads, a gibbet is believed to have been on this site in medieval days. A small stone, about 3ft in height, stands next to the sign, possibly a remnant of a barrow, long ago vanished.

To the south-east of the village, close to the road from Avening, is the Long Stone, one of Gloucestershire's best known megaliths. The stone is close to 8ft in height by 5ft in width. Two holes run through the stone, one near its base, the other about halfway up. About 12 yards away is a second stone, significantly smaller than The Long Stone, which has been incorporated into a dry stone wall. Consisting of oolitic limestone, it has been suggested that the stones are the remnants of a long barrow, the Long Stone being compared with the Tingle Stone at Gatcombe Park. There is no trace of a mound, however. As with so many of these ancient stones, there are folklore traditions associated with Minchinhampton's Long Stone, and years ago, infants were passed through the larger of the holes. This, it was believed, was a cure for smallpox and rickets. At home I have a photograph I took of my then-wife standing by the stone, dating from the mid-1980s, when we visited it together. I was a great one for visiting burial mounds and monoliths and used to persuade her to traipse along with me – an activity that, I venture to suggest, was not her preferred option. In an effort to inject a little humour into my pious admiration of the venerable stone she stuck her face up to the hole and grinned mirthfully. This drew an angry reprimand from me. No surprise, then, that her expression in the photograph I subsequently took is glum and dejected. Poor girl – she little deserved such an irritable and cantankerous husband!

Cherington is about a mile and a half south-east of the Long Stone. This village has several pretty cottages and a large green, on which is a drinking fountain, dating from 1875 and bearing the inscription 'Let him that is athirst, come'. Also, at the bottom of a steep gradient below the village, there is a lake called Cherington Pond. The Church of St Nicholas is mainly thirteenth century and has a Norman tub-shaped font with a low pedestal on a very large circular base. Above the north doorway is a stone, which Arthur Mee in his 1938 volume *The King's England: Gloucestershire* describes as 'strangely carved with what looks rather like lions shaking hands'.

Now we head in the general direction of Cirencester, having successfully scoured around the most interesting places in the Stroud district. Rodmarton is about two-and-a-half miles south-east of Cherington. In a field about half a mile on the Cherington side of the village there is a chambered long barrow, known as Windmill Tump, which dates from about 3000 BC. The mound, about 180ft long and 70ft wide, is clearly visible. Unfortunately for the casual observer, many of the barrow's most interesting features are not visible, however, having been covered in for their protection. Two chambers opening onto the sides are of particular – invisible – interest, entry being through 'port-hole' apertures. When this barrow was excavated in 1863 thirteen skeletons were found. In the late Neolithic period, for reasons not clear, barrows such as this were abandoned or blocked-up. Here the port-hole entrance to the south chamber was neatly blocked with dry stone walling.

At the actual village of Rodmarton there is a church with a spire, and several fine tombs in the churchyard, and overlooking the green there are some neat little cottages.

Thames Head is about three-and-a-half miles to the north-east on the A433, which at this point follows the course of the Roman Fosse Way. Despite the claims of one or two other locations, the true source of the River Thames is here at Thames Head. The actual source is at Trewsbury Mead, a pleasant walk northwards across the fields from the Thames Head Inn on the Fosse Way. There is a granite slab declaring the river's source at a damp patch of ground below a tree. Until 1974 there used to be a statue of Neptune, but after this was repeatedly defaced by vandals, it was moved to St John's Lock below Lechlade. R.C. Skyring Walters, in

Right: *The Long Stone. (photograph courtesy of J. Bolan.)*

Below: *Windmill Tump in Rodmarton.*

his 1928 book *Ancient Wells, Springs and Holy Wells of Gloucestershire*, states that the source of the river is actually variable – after heavy rain in winter springs appear in several points north of the declared source. He adds that 'Lyd Well', half a mile south of the Thames Head Bridge, may be taken 'as a fairly normal source of the Thames'. Certainly it is here that the river first takes the form of an appreciable water flow. The Thames Head Bridge is to be seen to the south-east of the 'official' Thames source. This once carried the Fosse Way over the Thames and Severn Canal, but the canal has been disused for a great many years and the bridge is now situated on a lay-by near the road. A plaque is fixed to the parapet. To the south-east of the Fosse Way is a group of buildings (now a private house) that are the remains of the old Thames Head Pumping Station. During the canal's existence water was pumped from a deep well to top up the level of the canal – water shortages on the summit level were a regular problem.

Coates is around a mile and a half north of Thames Head, and about 100 yards from the Coates to Tarlton road is the entrance to the Thames and Severn Canal tunnel, which runs underground for two-and-a-quarter miles before coming out at Sapperton. The Coates entrance is quite ornate, with columns and a rusticated archway.

To pass through the tunnel, which was first used in 1789, bargees would propel the boats by lying on their backs and pushing with their feet against the tunnel roof – an operation that took over three hours. The Thames and Severn Canal was opened in 1789, to link the Stroudwater Canal at Stroud with the Thames, near Lechlade. It was never a real success, and the tunnel, in particular, was always problematic. The canal closed in 1911.

Close to the Coates entrance is a public house, The Tunnel House Inn, which is full of character. Originally used as a resting place for bargees using the Thames and Severn Canal, the building is probably contemporary with the canal. I recall that when I called for some sustenance there in the 1980s a sleepy python was to be seen in a glass cabinet in the bar. The snake is no longer resident there, however, having been re-housed some years ago at the Cotswold Wildlife Park at Burford.

By road, Sapperton is about two-and-a-half miles north-west of Coates. It lies at the western edge of Cirencester Park and has a number of attractive buildings, as well as a good inn, The Bell. The church, mainly of the eighteenth century, has a number of items of interest, not least its monuments with life-size figures. The village is probably best known, however, for the afore-mentioned two and a quarter-mile canal tunnel that runs beneath the village, which, as already described, was opened in 1789 as a section of the Thames and Severn Canal. This linked the Stroudwater Canal at Stroud with the navigable Thames near Lechlade. At the time of the canal's opening, the tunnel – from Sapperton to Coates – was, at 3,817 yards,

*The canal tunnel entrance at Coates.*

the longest in England. The tunnel entrance is a little over 15ft wide, and the roof just over 10ft above the water. For over two miles the bargees lay on their backs and pushed with their feet against the roof to get through. For various reasons, however, the canal was never a success, the last recorded journey taking place in 1911. The Sapperton end of the tunnel is much less ornate than at the Coates end, but consolation can be had by visiting The Daneway Inn nearby. There are, apparently, serious plans to re-open the canal and the tunnel.

There are other tunnels of note at Sapperton. Two railway tunnels – one long and the other short – were opened by the engineer Isambard Kingdom Brunel in 1845, with a short section of daylight between the two. This section is easily visible from the Stroud to Cirencester road. The combined length of the two tunnels is 1,908 yards. The western end of the tunnels, where the line begins the descent through the Golden Valley, gives a good vantage point for trainspotters.

From Sapperton, we now follow the road north for about three miles until, at Jackbarrow Farm, a lane on the right leads to Duntisbourne Abbots. This village's name derives from its one-time ownership by the abbots of Gloucester. Small, neat and pretty, Duntisbourne has a saddleback-roofed church of Norman date. Below the church, beside the lane leading to Duntisbourne Leer, there is a well-head, which is the source of the Dunt stream. It once gushed into a massive stone trough, originally the village watering place. Now, however, the water runs into a large iron trough, only one end remaining of the stone trough. Five Mile House, next to the old Ermin Way, a little to the north-east of the village, is a pub that is full of character and charm, and has a reputation for serving very good meals.

Near the road, about a mile to the south of the village, is the Hoar Stone long barrow, about 120ft long by about 90ft wide. At the east end is a large stone, 12ft high and weighing between five and six tons, known as the Hoar Stone. It is thought that this stone may have formed a false portal. Another stone, about 9ft square, is situated to the south of the barrow's centre. Lying prostrate, it is believed to be the capstone of the mound's burial chamber.

Now we come to one of the major historical sites in the Cotswolds. About four miles south-east of Duntisbourne is Bagendon. This village is notable for the extensive system of ramparts and ditches, known as Bagendon Dykes. These are the remains of the Celtic tribal capital of the Belgic Dobunni, who inhabited much of Gloucestershire in the Iron Age, immediately before the coming of the Romans. These substantial earthworks are visible still as a deep and wide overgrown ditch to the east and south-east of the village, as one takes the narrow road from Woodmancote to Perrott's brook. Towards the south end the bank stands 5ft high. Excavations in the 1950s revealed the remains of stone-floored huts and imported pottery and glass, suggesting regular contact with the Roman Empire prior to the invasion of Britain. Far from being a tribe of savages, the Dobunni showed a high level of civilisation and there was evidence of an industrial establishment where iron, bronze and lead were worked, and silver coins were minted.

This is a very significant site, dating from about AD 25 or 30 to the Roman conquest, within fifteen years of which the Dobunni had become further Romanized – there was no sign of armed resistance at Bagendon – and migrated to the Roman city of Corinium at nearby Cirencester.

North Cerney is less than a mile north-east of Bagendon. This cheerful little village on the Churn not only has a good pub, The Bathurst Arms, but a fine twelfth-century church, where a search for curiosities will prove rewarding. Scratched onto the outer south wall below the transept window is a manticore, and a long-tailed leopard is on the west wall, on the lower part of the tower. Both, apparently, are a kind of graffiti left by Tudor masons. Quite apart from the 'curiosities' there is a great deal to see here, including a fifteenth-century pulpit, medieval glass and much else of beauty and intrigue.

*The village pump at North Cerney.*

At the corner of a road called 'Hill View', up the steep hill past the village school, stands an iron pump, surrounded by a structure of natural stone, quarried at Daglingworth. A number of holes can be seen in this stone, which, according to R.C. Skyring Walters in his 1928 book *Ancient Wells, Springs and Holy Wells of Gloucestershire*, were caused by '…worms burrowing in the then soft ooze or mud, which has since hardened and now constitutes stone…'

As at nearby Bagendon, there is substantial evidence of the Celtic tribal capital of the Dobunni. Extensive earthworks in the form of defensive ramparts and ditches can be seen close to Scrubditch Farm, where the bank still stands to a height of almost 10ft, these remains being probably the most visible signs of ancient occupation. Excavations revealed the remains of stone-floored huts, and imported pottery and glass, suggesting regular contact with the Roman Empire prior to the invasion of Britain. Additionally, there was evidence of an industrial establishment where iron, bronze and lead were worked, and silver coins were minted. This is a very significant site, dating from about AD 25 or 30 to the Roman conquest.

*Remnants of the Roman temple near Chedworth.*

There is a right-of-way running alongside Scrubditch Farm, but the earthworks are on private land, so permission should be sought before attempting to view them.

Just over a mile to the east, towards the Fosse Way, is Calmsden. This neat little hamlet on open country receives scant mention in the guide books, but has some early nineteenth-century estate cottages with glazed diamond or hexagonal window panes. Its village cross is particularly interesting, consisting of four steps, a stone base and a tall shaft. It dates probably from the early fourteenth century, and has been erected over a spring, the water from which discharges into an iron trough by the side of the road. The only later addition to the original structure is a cube dial.

For a while, now, we head towards the North Cotswolds. We head north-east from Calmsden on the A429 (Fosse Way) until, at the bottom of a dip called Fossebridge, we take a lane on the left to Chedworth Woods, where we find the lovely Chedworth Roman Villa. The journey from Calmsden is not far short of six miles. The Roman villa at Chedworth is very well known, often being described as among the most attractively sited villas in the country. Certainly its position, on a wooded slope of the Coln Valley, is indeed lovely. The villa, discovered in 1864 when a gamekeeper digging to retrieve a lost ferret discovered a mosaic pavement, was a large country house and dates from about AD 120-400. It is in the care of the National Trust, and there is much to see, including bath suites, mosaic pavements and a good museum.

It is probable that relatively few of the visitors to the villa at Chedworth will be aware that half a mile away, in the woods about 50ft above the River Coln, are the remains of a Roman temple. Excavations took place in 1864-5 and 1930, revealing that a massive artificial platform is a remnant of a 50ft square temple, which had been set on a podium of very large hewn limestone blocks. Archaeological finds included bones of red deer, a fragment of a capital, moulded stone architrave and hexagonal slates. Coins from the site suggested the temple may have been constructed in the second century AD. To be truthful, there is not a great deal to see now. Heavily overgrown with mature trees, bracken and brambles, the existing bank and mound do have a lot of stone spread about the surface, and in particular, several very large moss-covered stone blocks possibly form part of what was the podium.

Running through the middle of the wood, and passing close to the villa, is the course of the Midland and South Western Junction Railway's branch line from Andoversford to Swindon. The line was opened in 1891 and included construction of Chedworth tunnel, which is 491 yards in length and has a stone portal at the southern end, visible from the village. The line was particularly busy in the two world wars, carrying military supplies to the channel ports and hospital trains from Southampton to northern destinations. Subsequently becoming uneconomic, however, the line was closed in 1961.

A little to the south of Chedworth Woods, and visible from lanes that cross former runways, is the old wartime Chedworth airfield, which opened in 1942 as a satellite to the training unit at Aston Down. During 1942, Spitfires were based here for the training of squadron leaders, but in 1943 the airfield was being used for air gunnery training. 1944 saw Mustangs and Typhoon fighter-bombers at the airfield, but the airfield's active life ceased after the war and by the 1950s had come to the end of its life. Concrete and brick buildings remain on the north side, and a Blister hangar is still in good condition. A visit is certainly worthwhile for anyone interested in this period of our history.

About two-and-a-half miles north-east of Chedworth, and delightfully situated overlooking the woods of the Coln Valley, Yanworth has a small Norman stone-floored church, which retains several features from that period, including a south doorway with chevron moulding, its chancel arch and tub font. From a later period is a very interesting wall painting of a Father Time, depicted in skeletal form with scythe. This is believed to date from the late sixteenth century.

Some way from the centre of the village, near the old A40 road from Northleach to Cheltenham, is an interesting feature known as the 'Hangman's Stone'. The stone actually consists of two stones, one of which has been set into a dry stone wall for use as a stile. The main Yanworth stone can be seen nearby, lying on its side,

Above: *The 'Hangman's Stone'.*

Left: *The crocodile spring in Compton Abdale.*

close to the same wall. It is a rough-surfaced, holed slab of about 7ft in length. At its widest point it is a little less than 3ft, with the hole at its upper end. There is a folklore tradition that it takes its name from an incident in which a sheep rustler was hanged – when climbing over the stile, he became entangled with the sheep he was stealing. This yarn takes some believing, and as the stones are at the junction of the parishes of Yanworth and Hampnett, it is more plausible that they once marked the site of a gibbet.

From Yanworth village a very pretty, but somewhat circuitous, road takes us to the village of Compton Abdale. This is a very small village set in a valley. Several pretty houses and cottages are scattered about the place and there is a pleasant village hall. There is no pub or village shop, and the church interior is unexceptional – though the building does have a fine tower. Compton Abdale's most interesting feature is probably the spring and well, below the churchyard. The water gushes forth from the carved jaws of a crocodile into a large stone trough. To be honest, the crocodile is now virtually unrecognizable as such, the stone forming the snout having worn away and been patched up inexpertly. Even so, the well is a very unusual feature of the village.

The next 'stop' is at Withington, about a mile-and-a-half along a lane that leads south-west out of Compton Abdale. This quiet village has a lovely church with some fine old yews in the churchyard. A Norman building, the south doorway is especially well ornamented. There are other attractive buildings as well, not least the hospitable Mill Inn with the little River Coln flowing through its gardens. The King's Head, in King's Head Lane, is a friendly and traditional pub, serving local real ales.

On past the Mill Inn, and down Woodbridge Lane, towards the edge of Withington Woods, are the remains of the railway bridge on the Midland and South Western Junction Railway, which ran at this spot from 1891 to 1962. This section of the line was on the route from Cheltenham to Cirencester. It is a very quiet and picturesque spot and makes a pleasant walk.

Heading south again, now, we arrive at Rendcomb after about four-and-a-half miles. Here there is an attractive fifteenth-century church, which has a beautiful Norman font, with the carved figures of eleven apostles, with the figure of Judas left uncarved. The font is believed to have come from the village of Elmore, near Gloucester.

Of considerable historical interest at Rendcomb are the barely-recognizable remnants of a First World War airfield. Situated to the east of White Way, with the North Cerney to Calmsden road forming its southern edge, this was the base for 48 Squadron of the Royal Flying Corps, equipped with Bristol fighters. The aerodrome opened in 1916, remaining busy until its closure in 1920-1. Various First World War buildings, including a one-time rifle range, remain in the vicinity of Rendcomb Buildings, Rainbow Barn and Chalkhill Wood. These are all on private property, however, and permission should be obtained before any attempt is made to visit them.

Standing on the site of Roman Corinium, Cirencester – about five miles south of Rendcomb – is today a busy market town and centre for tourism in the area. Little of the old Roman city now exists, though there is a stretch of the Roman town wall – constructed in the mid- to late third century AD – on the side of the Abbey grounds and a large amphitheatre to the south of the ring road. The precise date at which the foundation of Corinium occurred is unknown. Archaeological research has shown, however, that the streets were laid out in the last quarter of the first century AD. It is thought that towards the end of the second century AD Cirencester became the capital of one of the provinces into which Britain was divided – indeed, it became the second largest city in Roman Britain – and it was during this period that construction of the amphitheatre took place, superseding a timber-built construction. Situated on the waste land of disused quarries, the quarry waste was used for the embankment, which formed the base for seats. The central area of the amphitheatre is elliptical, and when excavated in 1966, it was shown that there had been at least thirty rows of seats, accommodating about 8,000 people. Gladiators may have fought in the amphitheatre, but more commonly there would have been displays of bear-baiting and wrestling and it would have been used as an assembly point for the population to hear speeches from officials.

The town's history was relatively insignificant after the departure of the Romans, but it gained in wealth and importance in medieval times, as it became a centre of the wool and cloth trade. The splendid tower and porch of the Church of St John the Baptist, the largest of the wool churches, stands proudly over the market place. The origins of the church are in the twelfth century, though very little remains from that period. The Perpendicular tower was erected around 1460, the great south porch being added in 1490. After the Dissolution the church became the town hall, before being handed back to the vicar in the eighteenth century. There is a great deal to see in the church and especially do not miss the fifteenth-century pulpit of stone on a wineglass-shaped pedestal. There is a curiosity in the Lady Chapel, where there is a cat chasing a mouse – apparently a craftsman's joke.

Immediately west of the town is Cirencester Park. The house is not open to the public, but most of the great park is accessible to people on foot. The poet, Alexander Pope, spent a number of summers at the park in the first quarter of the eighteenth century, visiting his friend, the 1st Earl Bathurst and near the polo ground a rusticated shelter known as Pope's Seat can be seen. There are a number of other follies in the Park, including a castellated ruin called Alfred's Hall (the first castellated folly in England) and a Doric column, topped by a statue of Queen Anne, which was erected in 1741. It is easy to spend an entire day in Cirencester. The Corinium Museum in Park Street is thoroughly interesting and there are lots of inviting shops, as well as a number of good pubs and restaurants. Easily the best pub in town, though, is The Twelve Bells in Lewis Lane.

It has a constantly-changing range of real ales, and serves excellent food. When based at the nearby police station in the late 1990s I soon found out that it was an excellent place to visit for lunch. By this time I was in the twilight years of my police service and worked in plain clothes as a Crime Prevention Officer.

If we now take the A419 south-east out of Cirencester, then follow the road towards South Cerney, we find a turn on the right leads into Siddington. On the edge of Cirencester, this village is on the course of the Thames and Severn Canal, but this waterway was closed in 1911. There is a pleasant Norman church here, noted for its tympanum and south doorway. Next to the churchyard is a sixteenth-century barn.

Near the road to South Cerney there is a curious castellated tower. This folly dates from the eighteenth century and may once have been a windmill – which possibly accounts for the local belief that it was built by a Dutchman who settled in the area. The tower is somewhat dilapidated though; at the time of writing, remedial work is being undertaken.

Now we need to turn around and return to the A419, before turning off for Preston. From Preston we follow Witpit Lane north to join the A417, then turn right to head for Ampney Crucis – a journey of about three miles. Situated at the side of the A417 road, Ampney Crucis is the largest of three 'Ampney' villages on the Ampney Brook outside Cirencester, all of which are worth a visit. A lane leading from the main road into the village crosses a five-arched stone bridge, with the nearby mill standing at the edge of the brook.

The village has several attractive stone cottages and a picturesque church with features that date from the Saxon period right up to the nineteenth century. On the north of the nave is a Saxon doorway – tall and narrow, with a flat head formed of two massive lintels – and the Norman chancel arch, resting on carved capitals, is particularly impressive. The Perpendicular stone pulpit, of polygonal design, is noteworthy, as is the sixteenth-century tomb of George and Annie Lloyd, their five sons and seven daughters kneeling around them.

In the north transept are the remains of an early fourteenth-century wall painting depicting the figures of saints and the arms of Fitzhamon of Tewkesbury (the

*The elevated pump in Meysey Hampton.*

manor at that time belonged to Tewkesbury Abbey). In the churchyard is a fifteenth-century cross with a gabled top, rediscovered in 1854 having been built into
the rood loft stair.

At Ampney Park there is a fascinating garden maze in the shape of a giant foot.
Named 'Imprint' and planted in 1975, it was designed by Randoll Coate after the
Park's owner said he wished to leave his mark on the land. The giant foot is actually
a composite, formed by the tracing of the left foot of each member of the family. The tracings were then merged to form a single foot. The maze is filled with
birds, frogs, snakes and other creatures, as well as planets and the signs of the zodiac.
Ampney Park is occasionally opened to the public for charity events and the like.

Less than a mile from Ampney Crucis is Ampney St Mary's church. The actual
village is about a mile north of its original site on the Ampney Brook, having
uprooted many years ago to the hamlet of Ashbrook, probably because of a combination of the Black Death and repeated flooding of the village. There is little to
see at the village itself, but a number of interesting features can be seen at the little
Church of Saint Mary, which stands isolated in a meadow between the A417 road
and the Ampney Brook.

The church dates from the early twelfth century, chief among its notable posses-
sions being some striking medieval wall paintings. One illustrates St Christopher,
another St George and the Dragon, but the most interesting and best preserved is

a fourteenth-century illustration of how labour on a Sunday wounds Christ. The wounds to his body, together with the implements of manual labour that inflicted them, are graphically depicted.

The Norman lintel over the north doorway is of special interest. The Lion of Righteousness is shown triumphing over the forces of evil, here represented by two coiled, snake-like bodies. The floor is of stone slabs, adding to the timelessness and peaceful atmosphere. The Church of Saint Mary is locally called the Ivy Church, from when it was disused between 1879 and 1913, standing alone in a condition of ivy-clad decay.

Close to the A417 road, and a near neighbour to Ampney St Mary and Ampney Crucis, Ampney St Peter consists mainly of a small cluster of cottages around a triangular green. It has a small church with a saddleback tower and a late Saxon nave, a spacious north aisle dating from rebuilding and restoration in 1878. This is a light and cheerful little building, one feature being of particular interest. This is a nude female figure – thought to be a fertility symbol of Saxon origin – overlooking the font. In the churchyard are the remains of a fourteenth-century cross.

The earthworks known as Ranbury Ring, the remains of an Iron Age hillfort, are on ground to the south east of the village. An outer bank and ditch encloses an 11½ acre site.

The ancient village pub, The Red Lion, is worth a visit. It is a bit like stepping back in time, though. There are two tiny bars with stone floors, and the beer is good. You cannot get food, however – this is strictly a pub for the thirsty only.

To get to the next 'stop' we continue east along the A417 for about three miles, until we reach the village of Meysey Hampton. Here there is a thirteenth-century church, a Georgian manor house and a good pub, The Mason's Arms. For a short time in 1981 it became my regular watering-hole when I became acquainted with a young lady working as an au pair in the village, so you would be right to surmise the place holds fond memories for me. There is a post office and village shop, too, with free internet facilities on offer.

The church has some good sculpture work and some interesting monuments. It is in a particularly pleasing situation, the churchyard overlooking a large pool, with reeds, rushes and quacking ducks. Two benches have been provided, and the banks were covered with snowdrops when I visited. A small stone building in the corner of the churchyard is particularly interesting. This was at one time used as a watch house to guard against bodysnatching from new graves.

The village has a neat, semi-circular green close to the pub, upon which there is a pump raised above the ground. It is reached by a flight of stone steps leading up to it, and was originally used to fill casks carried on horse-drawn farm wagons. About a mile and a half further east is Fairford. This town on the River Coln flourished in medieval times due to the wealth of the Tames – a great wool merchant family – and it was their wealth that paid for the building of the impressive fifteenth-century church, with its massive central tower and lovely original stained-glass windows. The tower is covered with a number of interesting grotesques as well as unusual sculptures that include a griffin and a muzzled bear. In the churchyard there are several interesting table-tombs, including one with 'Egyptian' caryatids (female figures used as supporting pillars).

Also in the churchyard, near the porch, is an unusual memorial. It is engraved:

TIDDLES

THE CHURCH CAT

*1963-1980*

Apparently the verger took pity on a half-starved stray kitten he found in the churchyard in 1963. The cat went on to spend the next seventeen years at the church, becoming well-liked by the congregation, who grew used to Tiddles settling on any convenient lap during sermons. When Tiddles died in 1980 a local stonemason carved the unusual stone memorial.

The rest of the town is not without interesting buildings and there are a number of old hotels and inns worthy of a visit. And now we head for border country again.

Three miles east of Fairford, Lechlade is a small town close to the borders with Wiltshire and Oxfordshire. It takes its name from the River Leach, which, together with the River Coln, joins the Thames here. And it was from here that stone quarried in the Burford area, and used in the building of fine buildings in London and Oxford, was shipped down river. When the Thames and Severn Canal was opened in 1789 it was also possible to load stone from narrow boats using the canal on to vessels navigating the Thames.

Lechlade is still busy with boats, though nowadays, of course, for pleasure only. The town has a number of interesting buildings and a fine Perpendicular church. There are a couple of notable bridges – Ha'Penny Bridge, with its small square tollhouse, at the southern end of the town, and St John's Bridge in meadows to the south-east. St John's Bridge is particularly significant. It had been built by 1228, and carried the main road from mid-Gloucestershire to London. It was rebuilt in around 1831, and was altered again in 1884. The name of the bridge comes from the Augustinian hospital, founded on the site now occupied by The Trout Inn – keen-eyed television viewers may have seen fictional detective Inspector Morse

*The twelfth-century font in the Church of St Peter, Southrop.*

taking a pint or two here. St John's Lock marks the highest navigable reaches of the Thames.

To get to Southrop, about three miles north-west of Lechlade, involves sneaking temporarily over the Oxfordshire border, just passing the edge of Little Faringdon. And we've only really come here to see a font. But what a font!

Behind the manor of this village beside the River Leach is the small Church of Saint Peter, which contains what is generally regarded as the finest example of Norman craftsmanship in the Cotswolds.

The building has a Norman chancel arch and finely moulded north doorway, but it is the twelfth-century font, of creamy white stone, that attracts most attention. Carvings in a series of eight arches below the tub-shaped bowl depict Moses with the Tablets of the Law and the Virtues - here shown as warrior females - trampling on the Vices. The Virtues have their names carved in the arches over their heads, while the names of the Vices are shown beneath, written backwards. Richly decorated, it is one of the finest fonts in Gloucestershire. Apparently, the font had for many years been built into the south doorway, but was rediscovered by John Keble, who was curate at Southrop for a short period in the 1820s.

Heading north once more, the next village on the 'tour' is Aldsworth – some eight miles or so north-west. This sleepy village lies just off the B4425 road between Cirencester and Burford, and the pretty Church of St Bartholomew can be seen perched on a hill above the village stream. The church has an imposing display of

*The former village lock-up, Bibury.*

gargoyles and a fine oak door, which has been turning on its original iron hinges for hundreds of years. The stone gargoyles are among the finest examples in the Cotswolds and can be seen above the north wall as one approaches by the path up the hill. Described in Arthur Mee's *King's England: Gloucestershire* as 'nightmares in stone', these sixteenth-century grotesques include men with their faces hideously contorted, dragons, and other bizarre images of horror and mirth.

The precise age of the north porch door is open to conjecture, but it is certainly very old and still has its original ironwork. Numerous books and guides have stated that the door is the original Norman structure, some 800 years old. Recent opinion, however, places its age nearer to 400 years. Whichever assertion is correct, it is certainly a fine example of carpentry, and together with the array of gargoyles, provides Aldsworth with some interesting curiosities.

Aldsworth is such a peaceful and law-abiding place that I rarely had occasion as a policeman to attend an incident there. On one occasion, however, I responded to a report from a young lad who had found hundreds of pounds in cash, scattered along the verges of the A433 road near the village. Despite publicity and appeals for the loser to come forward, no one ever did, and the boy was able to claim the cash – a just reward for exceptional honesty.

The village of Bibury is just over three miles to the south-west. As has been said by many a writer, Bibury is a beautiful village. On a sunny day in the holiday

*The fourteenth-century priest's house doorway.*

season, however, the place is absolutely swarming with visitors, and this does tend to detract from its charm. To see it at its best, then, it is recommended that a visit be made in spring or autumn, preferably on a weekday.

Situated on the River Coln, the village has plenty of attractions on offer. The Swan Hotel is a pleasant building and hostelry, and is a good place to commence a wander around Bibury. On the roadside next to the hotel is a small, hexagonal, windowless building with a heavy, studded oak door, which is kept locked. This was the village lock-up, built in the eighteenth century, its presence supporting a tradition that the manor court used to be held at the Swan.

An interesting museum is housed in Arlington Mill, while the nearby Bibury Trout Farm offers the opportunity to observe and feed the trout. Otters have in recent years returned to the River Coln and play havoc with the fish, much to the distress of the proprietors, though the sight of an otter is an enjoyment to many.

The village has a number of pleasant cottages overlooking its square, but the most attractive dwellings are to be seen at the delightful Arlington Row, owned by The National Trust and actually part of the separate hamlet named Arlington. None of these seventeenth-century weavers' cottages is open to the public, which is probably no bad thing. Close to Arlington Row is a water meadow named Rack Isle. The unusual name of this meadow refers to the days when it was a drying ground for cloth woven in the cottages and fulled at the mill opposite.

Following the lovely River Coln, we now head north-west for about three miles, until we arrive at Coln Rogers. This little village possesses a church that is unique in the Cotswolds. Set amid the water meadows of the Coln, the Church of St Andrew has a Saxon nave and chancel that have largely escaped 'restoration', and in the north wall of the nave a blocked doorway indicates elements of three architectural styles – Saxon, late Norman and Early English. Worth noting, too, is the small round-headed Saxon window in the north wall of the chancel, and the medieval oak chest with original ironwork. In a north window of the nave may be seen a tiny fifteenth-century figure in old glass of St Margaret with a book and rosary in her hands, and the head of a dragon beneath her feet.

Interesting features in the grassy churchyard include a beautiful modern gravestone to Professor David Talbot Rice in spangled Purbeck stone. This is by Simon Verity, whose statue of Daphne can be seen at Batsford Arboretum. Additionally, there is a memorial to twenty-five men and one woman who went off to the First World War and returned safely.

A little to the west of the church is a particularly interesting 'cowshed'. Believed to be a fourteenth-century priest's house, it still has a lovely arched doorway and is worth seeking out.

Now, about four miles to the north-east, we come to our last 'stop' in what I have termed the 'South Cotswolds'. Most would say that Eastington is actually in the North Cotswolds, and I cannot deny that it sits uncomfortably when lumped in with villages in the South Cotswolds. But there had to be a dividing line, of course, so there's your explanation.

The River Leach flows beside the road in this little hamlet near Northleach, adding to the charm of the Cotswold stone barns and cottages. To the north-east of the hamlet is Upper End, where there is a delightful manor house and dovecote, both of which belonged to Gloucester Abbey before the dissolution. The dovecote is a circular building with a conical roof, and lantern. It may date from as early as the fifteenth century.

# 3

# WORCESTERSHIRE AND WARWICKSHIRE COTSWOLDS

Having navigated the hills and valleys of the South Cotswolds, we now turn our attention again to the north, though this time we will look at villages in Worcestershire and Warwickshire. The purists, of course, may well say there are few Cotswolds villages in Warwickshire, and still fewer in Worcestershire. Well, I don't believe in being too pedantic about this, but surely it can be agreed that Bredon Hill (Worcestershire) and Meon Hill (Warwickshire) are 'Cotswolds' hills? And who could argue that Broadway and Long Compton do not have all the characteristics of Cotswolds villages? I remember that, as a child in Wales, I was assured by an elderly neighbour that he was from 'the Cotswolds'. I subsequently found out that he was actually from the Vale of Evesham. Did it really matter? No, of course not. And so, then, we will press on regardless.

The Cotswold outlier of Bredon Hill is actually within Kemerton Parish, in Worcestershire, though it is close to the junction of Gloucestershire, Warwickshire and Worcestershire. On the northern slope approaching the hill there is a well called St Catherine's Well. A stream fed by the well trickles gently down the slope of the hill, and by following it to its source, St Catherine's Well can eventually be found. Consisting simply of a single stone trough measuring about 8ft long by 3½ft wide, and 2½ft deep, there are a few letters or marks along the rim at one end, though these are not readily decipherable. The well is fairly easily reached, being situated below the steepest part of the hill and though the ground round about is uneven and littered with rocks and stones, it is not particularly steep.

The hill reaches 1,000ft above sea level and is crowned by an impressive Iron Age fort dating from the second century BC. It has two formidable lines of ramparts on the south and east, with a steep drop on the other sides. During archaeological examination a number of skulls, bearing signs of violent attack, were found at the entrance, where there would have been wooden gates. The likelihood is that the tribe holding the fort had displayed the heads of their enemies on the gates.

*Bredon hillfort and Parson's Folly.*

On the highest point of the hill, and within the Iron Age hillfort, stands a square stone tower known as Parson's Folly. It was built in the eighteenth century by a squire of that name from Kemerton, apparently as a summerhouse. An array of aerials on its roof leads one to assume that nowadays it houses some kind of electrical or communications apparatus. Certainly entry is not permissible.

Close to Parson's Folly lies a large uncut limestone boulder that originally stood higher up the hill. Apparently it overbalanced and tumbled down the slope countless years ago, coming to rest in several pieces. The main stone is about 20 yards in circumference and 4 yards high, and no doubt weighs hundreds of tons. Known locally as 'The Elephant Stone', it does indeed resemble a kneeling elephant when viewed from a certain angle. O.G.S. Crawford, however, in his book *Long Barrows of the Cotswolds*, states that the stone '… looks something like the hull of a ship coming out of dock.' Whatever it resembles, it is probably an erratic deposited during frost heave in the glacial periods.

I well remember climbing to the top of this magnificent hill in the early 1990s. It was quite soon after I'd been diagnosed with MS and I think perhaps I needed some time alone, as well as having a point to prove to myself. It was a glorious day and, despite a few minor struggles, I got to the top and gazed out over the Vale of Evesham beyond. What a good feeling that was! Now, many years later, I've slowed up a bit, but still get great pleasure from the Cotswolds and its many beautiful views.

The village of Elmley Castle is at the foot of Bredon Hill. There is very little to be seen of the Norman castle, from which this pretty village takes its name. Built in

1086, it had become dilapidated by the fifteenth century, and its stone was used by local builders to construct other dwellings. Its surviving earth ramparts and ditches can be seen at Castle Hill on the north-east slopes of Bredon Hill, about half a mile south of the village.

The Norman church is very interesting. There are several curious carvings, including a rabbit and a pig, on the stone walls of the porch. The font is partly thirteenth-century, its base carved with dragons and its bowl – a later addition – carved on eight sides with wounds of the Lord. In the churchyard are two sixteenth-century sundials.

A curiosity of a different kind existed at Elmley Castle until the last decade of the twentieth century. A 'cider house' called The Plough was widely known among connoisseurs of the drink for its particularly potent cider. Before it finally closed its doors I visited the establishment to try the cider for myself. It was an unusual place – several addled-looking 'biker' types were seated outside and were either mumbling incoherently or staring vacantly into space – and I was required to pay a returnable deposit on my glass before being served with any cider. Actually, when I tasted it, it was quite pleasant and not obviously powerful. One of the bikers advised me that the stuff was very deceptive and that after a couple of pints the uninitiated invariably collapsed when they came to leave. Wisely, I think, I drank my half-pint and departed.

Leaving Elmley Castle, we follow the road east, past Hinton-on-the-Green, until we reach Childswickham. There we turn left along Murcot Road, arriving at the A44, a little to the south-east of Wickhamford – a distance of about eight miles. It is probable that most motorists do not stop at the village, except perhaps to buy some produce from one of the excellent roadside farm shops or call in at the useful post office and village store, but it is well worth turning off the main road to see the old part of the village (where there is a good pub named Sandys Arms) and to visit the delightful little Church of St John the Baptist.

The chancel is mainly thirteenth century, and there is an unusual medieval three-decker pulpit. Particularly interesting, however, is a floor-slab memorial behind the altar rails. It is dedicated to Penelope Washington, who died in 1697 and was an ancestral relative of George Washington, the first president of the USA (1789 to 1797). Penelope was the daughter of Colonel Henry Washington, who fought for Charles I at Worcester.

I had occasion to visit Wickhamford fairly regularly during my time as a North Cotswolds policeman. Whenever a stray dog was brought to the station – which was quite frequently – it would, after a few hours of fruitless efforts to trace an owner, be taken to the National Canine Defence League's kennels complex at

Wickhamford. The dogs I transported could be large or small, aggressive or docile. They were generally fairly quiet on the journey, but on a few occasions the entire trip was accompanied by howls and snarls. Certainly I remember stopping once to try and pacify a particularly troublesome hound, and, as soon as I opened the tailgate, it bolted – never to be seen again.

Now we need to head for the village of Bretforton, a couple of miles to the north-east of Wickhamford. Here we find the attractive timber-framed Fleece Inn building, a National Trust property that offers an excellent range of real ales, as well as good food and regular folk evenings. Little altered by the passage of time, the entire building will appeal to those in search of curiosities. Of particular interest, however, are some ancient circles that can be seen on the hearth in two of the inn's rooms. Known as 'witch marks', these were regularly drawn in groups of three, using white chalk. An old superstition states that witches may enter a house through a chimney, but that the circles would prevent them from going any further. The number three was considered sacred, the colour white symbolized purity and the circle has long been considered a symbol of eternity and perfection. The custom of drawing these circles is still kept up, centuries of this practice having left indentations in the stone. Despite the presence of the circles, however, misfortune befell the inn during early 2004, when a major fire caused substantial damage to the place. Fortunately, complete renovation has taken place and in the summer of 2005 the inn – if anything, in an improved condition – was once again opened to the public.

And now, after a trip of about five miles to the south-east (and passing through the Gloucestershire villages of Weston Subedge and Willersey), we come to our last stopping place in Worcestershire. The pretty village of Broadway, with its mellow Cotswold stone cottages and houses, is positioned at the edge of the Vale of Evesham, just below the Cotswold escarpment known as Fish Hill.

Its appearance is more 'Cotswold' than 'Vale', however, and it is one of the area's main 'show' villages, always busy with tourists. In Church Street there is an excellent seventeenth-century pub, The Crown and Trumpet. Full of character, this hostelry provides good food and fine ales from the Stanway Brewery. As well as the many fine buildings, Broadway has several curiosities that are worth making a special effort to see. Each of them, however, is a little way out of the village centre.

First visit Broadway's old Church of St Eadburgha, situated some way along the lane leading to Snowshill. This is the village's original Norman church and should not be confused with the nineteenth-century Church of St Michael, nearer to the village. With a mainly twelfth-century chancel, fourteenth-century transepts and Norman tub font, the building's interior is unspoilt and peaceful, and looks out over a small tributary of the River Avon at the bottom of the churchyard. There is

*The Fleece Inn, Bretforton.*

a good mounting block with stone steps by the churchyard wall. Also in the building is an unusual bier with solid wooden wheels, presented to the church in 1888 in memory of Charles Smart, who had been vicar there for twenty-five years. The alms box, too, is very unusual, being fitted with three locks – one for the vicar and one for each of the church wardens.

The next three curiosities are at the top of Fish Hill, overlooking Broadway. Close to the A44 road, almost opposite a picnic area, is the building that was formerly the Fish Inn – in its later years a popular haunt for motorbike enthusiasts. It ceased trading in the 1980s and was originally a gazebo and summerhouse on the Earl of Coventry's estate overlooking Broadway. Reputedly haunted, it has an interesting sundial on its roof and a stone mounting block with steps outside. Years ago, the main road down the hill into Broadway ran alongside the inn, though subsequent changes to the highway mean that the road past the inn now comes to a dead end.

Nearby is the Broadway Tower Country Park, which offers an opportunity to visit other curiosities on the hillside. A landmark for miles around, Broadway Tower consists of a central tower with three small round outer towers. It is 55ft high and stands at 1031ft above sea level. Designed by James Wyatt, it was built in 1796 by the 6th Earl of Coventry as a shooting box, probably to celebrate the centenary of his Earldom (though some accounts state that the Earl built it for his wife). After renovation work in 1827 it became a dwelling house and on occasions in the

1870s craftsman and social reformer William Morris temporarily established himself there. The tower was actually lived in until about 1972, the last occupant having lived there for forty years – without electricity or telephone, and with very little water. During the Second World War the Royal Observer Corps used the topmost storey as an observation post, and one can imagine that the Coventry blitz of 1940 would have been clearly visible. The tower is now open to visitors as part of the country park, and houses exhibitions and a gift shop. It has been claimed that on a clear day thirteen counties can be seen from the tower, with the notable buildings of Warwick Castle, Tewkesbury Abbey and Worcester Cathedral being discernible.

A memorial stone to an air crew killed nearby can be seen a little way down the grassy hill from the tower. In June 2000 the stone was unveiled to mark the spot where on 2 June 1943 a Whitley 5 plane from nearby Honeybourne airfield crashed, killing two Canadian and three British servicemen. The plane had been on a training exercise and had encountered heavy rain and mist, hitting the hill about 200 yards from Broadway Tower. Two men from the Royal Observer Corps post at the tower rushed to help the crew, but all had been killed except the rear gunner, who died soon after. In pulling him out of the burning fuselage the Observer Corps men had shown great bravery, subsequently receiving a certificate of appreciation from the Prime Minister, Winston Churchill.

The next 'stop' is at Lower Quinton in Warwickshire. This, I am afraid, involves a drive of about eight miles. I suggest taking the A46 north out of Broadway, then drive through Willersey and Weston Subedge, and thence to Mickleton before arriving at Lower Quinton. With its black and white timbered cottages, this is barely a 'Cotswold' village, but the dark hill that looms over the place might be considered as the last outpost of the Cotswolds. The last Cotswold hill in the northern-most tip of the region, Meon Hill, can be seen for miles around. The summit bears the clear outline of the ramparts of an Iron Age hillfort, best seen on the south-west, and in 1824 several hundred iron currency bars were found. The hill became notorious in 1945 when an elderly hedge-cutter was found murdered on its slopes, a hay-fork having been driven into the ground, so that the tines were either side of his neck, pinning him down. The shape of a cross had been hacked into his chest, the murder weapon left embedded in his trunk. It soon gained a reputation as a 'witchcraft murder' and to this day remains unsolved – though amateur sleuths still visit Lower Quinton occasionally, hoping to unearth some new clue.

I have to admit that when I first arrived in the North Cotswolds in 1981 I soon became a little obsessed with the murder after hearing local assertions about the killer's identity. Wanders around Lower Quinton and Meon Hill achieved nothing, of course, and when my research suggested that the local 'sages' were probably right,

*Meon Hill from the churchyard in Lower Quinton.*

I felt I had gone about as far as I could. I subsequently wrote what I believe to be a fair summary of the case in my 1993 book *Folklore and Mysteries of the Cotswolds.*

Leaving behind tales of murder and mystery, we head east out of Lower Quinton and drive the three-and-a-half miles to Crimscote. We drive north through the village until, after about a mile, Whitchurch Farm is found on the right. Here, we have to walk for a few hundred yards. There is no longer a hamlet of Whitchurch but the 'white church' of Saint Mary the Virgin still stands on the site of the former village, on a piece of raised ground in the meadows next to the meandering River Stour. The hamlet disappeared in the late fifteenth century, following depopulation, but though there is no road or electricity, services by candlelight continue to be held at the church.

Much of the building is of interest, with the west window memorial to baby Harry Rutter, dedicated in 1989, striking an especially poignant note. The church-yard itself is particularly evocative, with many of the ivy-clad tombs creating an atmospheric and timeless setting.

Now we return to Crimscote, and on to the A34, where we turn left and drive for a very short distance in the direction of Stratford-upon-Avon. Ettington Park Hotel – a grand residence set in lush parkland – will be seen in fields on the right, close to the River Stour. The hotel has a long-standing reputation as a haunted house, and in 1963 its Gothic façade was used for the film *The Haunting.*

Across the lawn of the hotel is the ruin of Ettington's Norman church. In a buttress of the old nave there is a piscina shaped with a trefoil arch. Four stone angels

*The churchyard tombs at Whitchurch.*

look down from what was once a balcony, and on the lawn is an old stone which marks the boundary of what was the churchyard. This is an evocative ruin and merits a visit.

Just before arriving at Ettington Park, we took the lane from Crimscote to join the A34. The next point of interest is at this junction. This is the northern end of Newbold-on-Stour, a village with quaint old cottages and a fifteenth-century church, and though the busy A34 road cuts through its centre, the village is pretty enough. Standing at this junction is Newbold's most interesting curiosity – an elaborate milestone, approximately 8ft tall. Dated 1871, it bears the following inscriptions:

Facing Newbold:

*6 miles to Shakespeare's town whose name*
*is known throughout the Earth*
*To Shipston 2; whose lesser fame*
*Boast's no such poet's birth*

Facing Stratford:

*After darkness LIGHT*
*From light hope flows*
*And Peace is death.*
*In CHRIST a sure repose*

Many of the motorists who pass by this stone on the edge of the village, as they accelerate towards Stratford-upon-Avon, will be unaware of its existence. It is worth taking time to stop and appreciate the work that has gone into constructing this peculiar landmark. Standing either side of the road through the centre of the village are a couple of very good pubs, too: The White Hart and The Bird in Hand. Worth mentioning, as well, is a very useful village post office and stores nearby.

Less than a mile directly south of Newbold is Armscote. This little village just inside Warwickshire has a very 'Cotswold' feel to it, with its mellow stone cottages and Jacobean manor house. There is actually very little here, though the inn The Fox and Goose – better known to many Cotswold residents by its former name of The Wagon Wheel – is warm and hospitable.

Beside the road towards Halford, however, there is a 'building' that is quite a curiosity. What at first glace appears to be a bright and cheerful little bungalow, complete with pitched roof, chimneys and a wooden veranda, is actually a pair of old railway carriages. Actually, they aren't strictly a pair. Dated from about 1884, one originated from the Taff Valley Railway, the other from the Brecon and Merthyr Railway. They were purchased in 1928 for the princely sum of £12 each and converted into a dwelling, having been brought from nearby Shipston-on-Stour. The carriages, with their opening glass door panels, leather pull-straps and solid brass handles, were lived in by the same people for more than fifty years. The property was sold in the 1990s and the new owner built a house to the rear of the carriages, but far from consigning them to a bonfire, he carefully restored them so that today they stand as items of considerable interest to anyone who recognizes the 'bungalow' for what it really is.

There is much to commend Ilmington, about a mile and a half south-west of Armscote. Lying beneath the northern tip of the Cotswolds, this is a very pleasant village, with pretty stone cottages and houses, and a Norman church with some fine oak pews, installed in the 1930s. The pews are the work of master-craftsman Robert Thompson, whose unique trademark is a mouse, discreetly carved on everything he produced. The Ilmington pews each bear a little mouse.

There is an excellent inn in the village. With flagstone floors and a log-burning fire, The Howard Arms is every bit the traditional Cotswold inn. The place has a reputation for good food, and as well as guest beers, local ale brewed at nearby

*The direction stone, Newbold-on-Stour.*

Shipston-on-Stour is available. Looming above the village is Windmill Hill, which can be reached from a quiet lane that runs from Ilmington, across Ilmington Down, to Charingworth. This is a particularly peaceful spot, with fine views of the surrounding Warwickshire plains, and across to Edge Hill.

In the 1980s, when I was a policeman at Moreton-in-Marsh, I was called upon to go and regularly 'check' the radio masts at Ilmington whenever the police were placed on a higher-than-usual state of alert – generally because there had been major terrorist activity somewhere in the country. After dark, when the required check had been completed, I would often drive downhill to the west for a little under a mile to enjoy a viewpoint that offered a fine panorama over Mickleton, Long Lartin Prison and beyond to the Vale of Evesham. The viewpoint still exists, of course, though is not particularly well known.

About a mile and a half south-east, on the road to Shipston-on-Stour, is Darlingscott. It is pretty enough, but there is very little to see at this tiny village, and though there is a Victorian church with some nicely carved stonework, there is no pub and no shop. Until 1960 a railway branch line ran to the south of the village, Darlingscott's station being called 'Longdon Road'. The station was situated on the Moreton-in-Marsh to Shipston-on-Stour branch line of the Great Western Railway, which at this point used the old tramway line from Moreton-in-Marsh to Stratford-upon-Avon, which had opened in 1826. In 1918, however, any remaining

*The foundations of the Longdon Road railway station at Darlingscott.*

rails between Longdon Road and Stratford were lifted. The station consisted of a prefabricated wooden building on a single, short platform. The building was supported on brick arches, the line being built on an embankment at this point. The branch line closed in 1960, though it had been a freight-only service since 1929, and the station building had been taken down in about 1953.

The site of the station is today overgrown with trees, but traces of the platform can still be found among the undergrowth. The station building has, of course, long-since gone, but the brick arches that supported it can still be seen from an adjacent field. The next 'stop', about two miles to the north-east, is reached by taking the lane east to the A429, then north to Tredington. This village has a lot of modern housing and might at first glance seem a bit featureless, with its neatly manicured appearance. There are a number of impressive old houses, though, and the church is an exceptionally interesting building. It has a slender fifteenth-century spire, and there are remains of Anglo-Danish doors and windows above the present arcades between nave and aisles, about 13ft above the ground level. These date from before the Norman Conquest and are thought to be in this position so that the parson's entry to the church could be by ladder, his preaching taking place in the loft when hostile forces were in the area. The original building dates from about 1000, but the Norman additions and alterations date mainly from the twelfth, thirteenth and fifteenth centuries. The Jacobean pulpit is noteworthy and the old village stocks are kept in the building. The main door of the church bears the marks of bullets fired in the Civil War – seven bullets are still actually embedded in the wood.

Nearby, the pleasant village of Honington has an assortment of houses constructed of brick, stone and timber, as well as Honington Hall, which was built in 1685. A minor road leading off the A34 running between Shipston-on-Stour and Stratford-upon-Avon approaches the village after crossing the River Stour. The bridge over the Stour is exceptional. It has five arches, with ball finials on the parapet, and is thought to have been built in the 1670s or 1680s. It is worth climbing over the roadside fence and looking at the bridge from the riverbank, as the beauty of its design and antiquity cannot be properly appreciated from the road.

Shipston-on-Stour, the next 'stop', is easily reached, being less than a mile south of Honington. It has a number of pleasant houses, and there is a delightful little market square. Once an important market town for sheep, it is nowadays rather quiet. There are quite a few unusual and useful shops, however, and those with a thirst are well provided for. There are a number of welcoming pubs and inns – The White Bear, in the square, is especially good.

At Ditchford Farm, about a mile and a half to the south-west of the town, the North Cotswold Brewery was set up in 1999. A number of excellent beers, including 'Solstice' and 'Blitzen' are produced seasonally, with the curiously named 'Pig Brook' being the main regular ale. Twelve outlets are supplied direct.

Now heading east out of Shipston on the B4035 road to Banbury, Barcheston will be found on the right after half a mile or so. This is a tiny hamlet on the east side of the River Stour, with a manor house, a church and a rectory. Tapestry weaving was carried out at the manor house in the sixteenth century, and examples of the work can be seen at the York Museum and Oxford's Bodleian Library. Of most interest to the visitor, however, is Barcheston's church. The tower, more than 50ft high, leans over 20in to the west, but has done so for 500 years, so there is no cause for immediate alarm. Because of this list, however, the church bells can no longer be rung (though a striking mechanism is in use for chiming purposes).

Built between 1270 and 1280 on the site of an earlier building, the church has several unusual and curious features. In the south wall of the chancel there is a fine example of a priest's doorway, dated to the eleventh century and presumably a feature of the earlier building, which has been incorporated into the present church. The stone altar and font are both unusual and fine specimens. Additionally, there are several unusual medieval carvings: the green man at the entrance, the hand supporting the west end of the north arcade, the ram's head supporting the roof corbels and the human arms supporting the water spouts of the nave roof. The green man – or foliate head, to use its correct name – is particularly perplexing. Fairly common in

*The leaning church tower at Barcheston.*

the Cotswolds, and popular from early Christian times until the sixteenth century, the origin of foliate heads is thought to be Celtic. The purpose of the 'green men' is unknown, but the human head, swathed in foliage, is perhaps symbolic of the regeneration of the human spirit.

Continuing east along the Banbury road for around three miles, we arrive at Brailes. A lane leading north out of the village leads to Whatcote, and a substantial castle mound – its history lost in the mists of time – can be seen on the left. This can be reached by a public footpath leading off the road.

Upper Brailes virtually runs into Lower Brailes. The fourteenth-century church at this village is particularly notable, with a splendid tower and a nave containing eighteen corbel heads. There is much else to see, including a fourteenth-century font and a fifteenth-century chest, and in the porch there is a curious stone figure, originally from a tomb in the churchyard. The figure has been substantially worn by the effects of weathering, but at its feet is an animal. It is not readily discernible what this creature is, but in *The King's England: Warwickshire* Arthur Mee describes the figure as a 'proud man and his lion'.

The George Hotel is a lively inn with the excellent Hook Norton ales on tap. There are regular music evenings, with jazz and blues sessions.

The next site is so important, and affords such spectacular views, that the drive of around seven miles is surely worth the effort. As soon as we leave the houses of Lower

*The castle mound at Brailes.*

Brailes we must follow the narrow lane on the left, which leads to Winderton. Go through Winderton, turn right at the next junction, then, a short distance on, take the left turn towards Edgehill. For a short distance this run involves encroaching upon Oxfordshire, and the Second World War aerodrome of Edgehill – a satellite to the aerodrome at Moreton-in-Marsh – can be seen on ground to the right. A few wartime buildings still exist to the north of Rattlecombe Road, which leads to the village of Shenington. At a point just beyond the northern side of the aerodrome we are once again in Warwickshire.

The actual village of Edgehill is about two-and-a-half miles north-east of the former aerodrome. On the plain some 300ft below the ridge of Edgehill, a little to the north-west of the small village of Radway, the first major engagement of the first English Civil War took place on 23 October 1642. Though the battle saw 3,000 Royalist and Parliamentarian troops left dead or wounded, the campaign was not decisive and both sides fell back – the Royalists to Oxford and the Parliamentarians to Warwick. Over subsequent months and years much folklore built up around the battle, with claims of ghostly re-enactments taking place in the skies above Edgehill. Today, almost all of the battlefield site is Ministry of Defence property, but an excellent panoramic view can be had from Edgehill itself, the garden of The Castle Inn providing a good viewing point.

The Castle Inn itself is an octagonal castellated folly that was built in 1749 by Squire Sanderson Miller of Radway to commemorate the battle. Situated on the

*The view from Edgehill over the battlefield.*

spot where the king raised his standard, it consists of a gateway, bridge and tower with battlements. Inside the inn the walls of the main bar are decorated with weapons including swords and pistols.

A public footpath through Castle Wood, near the inn, passes close to an obelisk that overlooks the battlefield site. It was erected in 1854 by Charles Chambers to commemorate the battle of Waterloo.

Now, having feasted the eyes on the views from Edgehill, we have to head south again – this time for some eight or nine miles. Drive south-west past the former aerodrome, then, by-passing Epwell, go south towards Sibford Gower (we've crept into Oxfordshire again), then south-west to Whichford. This little 'trespass' into Oxfordshire has involved driving through some absolutely lovely countryside, but don't worry, we will return.

Whichford is a quiet village with a very large green. The green is overlooked by a splendid pub, The Norman Knight, where there is good food and a selection of fine ales, including 'Toad' and 'Druid's Fluid', brewed in adjacent premises. The Wizard Brewery began brewing here in 2003.

Having enjoyed an excellent beer at Whichford, why not have another – this time at our next stop, Little Compton? At Little Compton, just over five miles south-west of Whichford, The Red Lion serves ales from the Donnington Brewery, and the pub has a reputation for serving excellent food. Certainly it is very popular with diners and drinkers alike – unlike so many pubs that serve food, there is a real public bar.

There is, however, more to the village than the pub. There is a handsome seventeenth-century manor house, once the home of Bishop Juxon, who attended King Charles I at his execution. Today it is a college for accountancy. A view of the front of the house can be had through its front gates, next to the road and it can also be seen from the churchyard. Most of the church dates from the nineteenth century, but the fourteenth-century tower remains from the earlier building. The font, too, dates from the thirteenth century.

Late one evening in the early 1990s I was on police patrol in Moreton-in-Marsh when a very attractive young woman approached the police car and asked how to get to the college at Little Compton. Gallantly, I suggested she get into the car, and I drove her to the college. During conversation, it transpired that the lady was Russian and had earlier that day flown into Heathrow from Moscow. I never saw her again, of course, but I have occasionally wondered what she thought of the British police service.

There are a number of pretty cottages in the village and in spring the verges of the road leading up the hill to the Rollright Stones are brightly covered in daffodils, always a welcome sight.

Barton-on-the-Heath is about a mile and a half north of Little Compton. This is a quiet little village between Moreton-in-Marsh and Long Compton. The Church of St Lawrence is a pleasant Norman building, with a small saddleback tower, and a neat green overlooked by seventeenth-century Barton House. A pair of iron gates, dated 1986, at the start of the path leading up to the church are interesting and unusual, with decorations that include leaves, butterflies, birds and a horse. In the church a curious Norman carving of an animal – perhaps a pig – can be seen running up the chancel arch. Standing on the green is an interesting well-house with a stone dome supported by three columns.

Captain Robert Dover, who started the 'Cotswold Olympick' games near Chipping Campden, lived at Barton in the seventeenth century and is buried here, and William Shakespeare is thought to have used his knowledge of the village as the source of 'Burtonheath', mentioned in *The Taming of the Shrew*.

The next destination on the 'tour' is Long Compton, a mile and a half east of Barton-on-the-Heath. This village straggles along the busy A34 road and has a number of attractive cottages and houses. Much folklore surrounds the village and years ago it was supposed to be the haunt of witches. Indeed, in 1875 a local simpleton murdered an elderly woman in the village, apparently believing her to be a witch and the cause of many misfortunes. Thankfully, not too much witchery seems to go on today.

The church, with its fine Perpendicular tower, is very interesting. A stone female effigy in the porch is believed to be early fourteenth century. Very little detail remains, the stone having worn smooth over the centuries. It is likely that the stone at one time formed part of a tomb in the churchyard, though to whom it was a memorial is anyone's guess. Unsurprisingly, there is a story that this stone figure is that of a witch. In his 1968 book *Murder By Witchcraft* Donald McCormick describes how the female figure has '…an eerie and malevolent stare on her face… that fixed one at whatever angle one stood…' The author goes on to say that, even when moving back twenty paces from the figure, '…the stare was still directly confronting me.' Perhaps I'm a little less receptive to the malevolence of stone figures than some observers, but I have to say that I find Mr McCormick's description almost laughable. Still, perhaps the figure really is that of an eerie witch. Who knows?

The lychgate to the church forms an unusual entrance. The entrance was originally further west, and the lychgate was a small, two-storeyed cottage of the sixteenth century. The ground storey was removed to create the lychgate entrance, though when this took place cannot be ascertained. In the late 1950s the foundations of the building were being excavated during building work when a human skeleton was found 3ft down. Very old, it was taken to Warwick Museum, but was subsequently returned to the lych gate and in 1964 was interred inside the churchyard wall. Surprisingly, the building did not at that time belong to the church. A memorial stone fixed to the side of the building reads:

> George Kinsey Latham 1902-1964 bought and restored this building. It was given as a Memorial to him by his wife Marion
>
> 12.11.64.

Cherington is about four miles north of Long Compton, approached off the A34 to Shipston-on-Stour. Not a great deal about the village is exceptional, though it is a pretty enough little place and the fifteenth-century church does have some good stained glass windows – 'a charming coloured medley of sixteenth and seventeenth-century glass' says Arthur Mee in his 1936 volume *The King's England: Warwickshire*.

There is an excellent pub in the village, too. The Cherington Arms serves locally brewed Hook Norton ales and very good food, while maintaining its 'village pub' atmosphere. Interestingly, Cherington temporarily became 'Ambridge' village, from BBC Radio's long-running serial *The Archers*, in the late 1970s. Apparently there was a national competition to find the village that most resembled Ambridge, and Cherington was declared the winner. The village was filmed, with street and place names being changed, and The Cherington Arms temporarily became The Bull. It is likely that a number of towns and villages in this part of England provided

*The lychgate of the church at Long Compton.*

inspiration for locations in the serial. Certainly the village of Inkberrow, a few miles across into Worcestershire, lays claim to many 'Archers' connections.

The final 'stop' on this section of the Cotswolds is at Burmington Mill, about two and a half miles north of Cherington, just off the A34 towards Shipston-on-Stour. It ceased to be a mill more than fifty years ago, and was for many years used in connection with the building trade, then in 1991 became the Greenhill Christian Centre. It is open on Mondays and Saturdays, with beautifully crafted cards and works of art offered for sale. Additionally, there is a very peaceful dining and rest area, where refreshments are available. There is no actual charge for the refreshments, but donations can be placed in an alms box at the exit, should you wish. The place has a very happy and restful ambience and is an entirely appropriate place at which to conclude this section of the 'tour'.

# 4

# OXFORDSHIRE COTSWOLDS

Oxfordshire has, in my view, some of the loveliest Cotswold villages. The stone used in the building of the cottages is slightly darker than the pale Gloucestershire stone, but it is still very recognizable as oolitic limestone. The towns and villages in the Oxfordshire Cotswolds are to the north-east of the district and, though lying outside the area in which I was a policeman, are more familiar to me than, for example, villages in the Stroud area. Our starting point is, in fact, very near to Moreton-in-Marsh, where I did much of my police service.

Chastleton lies some three miles east of Moreton, about a mile along a lane leading off the A44 towards Chipping Norton. Dominating the small village is the beautiful Jacobean Chastleton House, built about 1603 by Walter Jones, a Witney wool merchant. The splendid building was for years in a condition of some neglect, but thankfully has now been restored to its former glory. In fact, I remember visiting the house in the 1980s, and, when I tried to open a back door to go in, the handle came off in my hand! Inside the house is the original wooden panelling and furniture, and there is a topiary garden of about 1700. Easily overlooked is the little eighteenth-century dovecote in a field opposite the house. In a lovely setting, overlooking the Evenlode Valley, it has a cupola and four gables standing on arches.

Taking the narrow lane past the house towards the main A436 Chipping Norton to Stow-on-the-Wold road, one is able to see a roughly circular Iron Age earthwork, less than a mile from Chastleton Village. It consists of a raised, stone-faced bank about 4ft high, covering an area of almost four acres. Parts of the bank are constructed of large limestone blocks, with fitted polygonal stones also having been found here. Known as Chastleton Barrow, the monument is just inside Oxfordshire, and unlike many of the hillforts in the Gloucestershire Cotswolds, is not in a naturally defensible position. Entrances have been identified on both the east and west sides, but the lack of any real evidence of settlement suggests that the earthwork was probably little more than a cattle pound or sheep-fold. Pottery found here dates from around the eighth century BC, and is now in the Ashmolean Museum at Oxford.

*The dovecote, Castleton.*

What is probably the most important historical monument in the region is the next item on the agenda. It is about three miles east, just outside Little Rollright. A seventeenth-century manor house, a few cottages and a church more or less comprise the village. The church has some fine seventeenth-century monuments and is worth visiting, but the village is mainly known for its ancient stones. Though of interest to the seeker of curiosities, the group of monuments known as the Rollright Stones is actually of major historical significance. The stones consist of three main elements:

(i) **The King's Men.** A ceremonial stone circle, dated about 2500-2000 BC. About 100ft in diameter, it consists of about 70 stones. Most are less than 4ft tall, but some are up to 7ft. The circle has long been associated with witchcraft and superstition. It can be seen next to the road between the A44 and the A34.

(ii) **The King Stone.** Just inside Warwickshire, across the road from The King's Men. A single stone monolith 8ft high and 5ft wide, it is thought to be a Bronze Age standing stone.

(iii) **The Whispering Knights**. Situated across a field from The King's Men, this monument consists of five large stones which are undoubtedly the remains of a Neolithic long barrow dated 3500-2500 BC.

Steeped in folklore, the monuments are the subjects of many improbable tales. One legend, in particular, explains their origin: a king and his men had arrived at Rollright on their way to conquer all of England, when they were suddenly confronted by a witch. Learning of the King's intentions, she announced:

Seven long strides though shalt take,
And if Long Compton thou can see
King of England thou shalt be.

The King replied:

Stick, stock, stone!
As King of England I shall be known.

The King then took the seven strides, but could not see the village of Long Compton in the valley below because a mound of earth rose up before him, obscuring his view. The witch then said:

As Long Compton thou canst not see
King of England thou shalt not be
Rise up, stick, and stand still, stone
For King of England thou shalt be none;
Thou and thy men hoar stones shall be
And I myself an eldern tree.

The hapless King and his men were thus turned to stone, along with a group of knights who had been whispering treacherously in the background. I have spent a number of happy hours at the stone circle formed by The King's Men. The monument used to be owned by a thoroughly interesting, and slightly eccentric, lady named Pauline Flick, with whom I was friendly. Sadly, she is no longer with us. Pauline was a great cat-lover and profits made from entrance fees were invariably donated to cats' welfare charities. She told me numerous interesting and amusing tales about the stones and their many peculiar visitors. Witches were regular visitors and Pauline once gave me the nod when a ceremony was planned to take place,

*The King's Men.*

in order that I could attend and make notes for a book I was then writing. The witches duly attended and performed their ceremony, though I sensed some were less than enthusiastic about my presence. Any hopes I may have entertained of witnessing nubile young women cavorting nakedly in the circle were soon dispelled, however. A particularly dark night, with lashing rain and swirling fog, rendered visibility almost non-existent.

If we now continue east past the stones, through nearby Great Rollright, we come to a left turn to Hook Norton – in total, the journey has covered about four miles. There is much of interest at this village. Together with its finely pinnacled Perpendicular tower, the church has a splendid Norman font with sculptured figures of Adam and Eve and signs of the Zodiac. This is a particularly fine example of Norman craftsmanship and should not be missed.

It is widely acknowledged among real ale enthusiasts that the beer brewed by the small family firm at Hook Norton is one of the finest ales in the country The brewery itself is an imposing example of a late Victorian tower brewery and is an impressive feature of the industrial history and architecture of the area. It is substantially constructed of brick, with local ironstone also having been used. The roof is of slate, while black and white half timbering and weatherboarding lend the building an attractive appearance. The original brewery was built in 1872, though substantial alterations and additions took place until completion in 1900. A faithful adherence to traditional brewing methods has ensured the retention of much of the original

*The Hook Norton brewery.*

machinery installed at the turn of the twentieth century, the brewery equipment and pumps still being powered by the original 25hp steam engine.

Between 1865 and 1889 the railway from Banbury to Cheltenham was constructed, passing through Hook Norton on its way to Chipping Norton. Together with a thriving local ironstone company, this contributed to the growth of the village as a centre of industry in the district. This boosted local demand for the ale, and though the railway and iron company have long since disappeared, Hook Norton ale continues in popularity throughout the area. It is possible to arrange public visits to the brewery. Nearby, too, is The Pear Tree Inn – a traditional village hostelry, serving local ales and good meals.

The Hook Norton section of the railway line was completed in 1889. Two spectacular viaducts were built between the village and nearby Great Rollright, spanning the valley between the station and the tunnel. These were substantial constructions (one of the viaducts had eight spans, and the other five) and 400 men were employed over the four years it took to build them, two workmen falling to their deaths during the construction work. In places the pillars were 90ft high, and it is these that remain, standing like sentinels in fields to the east of the village.

If we now drive north from Hook Norton, head west for Whichford, then take Traitor's Ford Lane north towards Sibford Ferris, we find ourselves passing through leafy woods and along a lane with high grass verges, upon which campion and cowslips grow freely – a welcome, and increasingly unusual sight. Sibford Ferris is about three miles from Hook Norton and is a pretty village, with mellow stone cottages. The road negotiates a steep slope bordered by fields of rough pasture, then leads into Burdrop, where, perched on a hill, is a fine seventeenth-century inn, The Bishop Blaize. The availability of good food and real ales make this a welcome stopping point.

Sibford Ferris virtually runs into Sibford Gower, where there is another welcoming hostelry, The Wykham Arms. This is a delightful Cotswold stone building, with a handsome thatched roof, where discerning diners are able to enjoy excellent food and wine in very welcoming and relaxed surroundings. Sibford Gower is a pretty little village of stone and thatch and has a nineteenth-century church with an interesting wall monument that resembles a small shrine. The artist Frank Lascelles chiselled a sculpture of his mother's face when she died, the miniature bust surrounded by alabaster flowers and gold mosaics. On the monument are Tennyson's moving lines:

Sleep sweetly, tender heart, in peace,
Sleep holy spirit, blessed soul,
While the stars burn, the moons increase,
And the great ages onward roll.

Sleep till the end, true soul and sweet
Nothing comes to thee new and strange.
Sleep, full of rest from head to feet;
Lie still, dry dust, secure of change.

An impressive bronze angel, fashioned by Lascelles, sits watching over the grave of his parents near the entrance to the church. Lascelles' artistic style is not to everyone's taste, but it is certainly striking. Also to be seen in the village, to the west of the church, is a Quaker burial ground. Peaceful and serene, with its memorial stones of uniform size and style, the ground has a meeting house nearby.

These villages are all perfectly charming, each having a good inn, and a drive around this part of the Cotswolds is very enjoyable. If we now take Pound Lane north out of Sibford Gower, we arrive at Epwell after just over a mile. This is another pleasant place, modern housing blending well with cottages of stone and thatch. The Chandler's Arms, serving Hook Norton ales, is a pretty little pub, welcoming and unpretentious. The village of Shutford lies a couple of miles east towards Banbury. Again, this is a lovely place, and there is yet another excellent hostelry. The

*The Bronze Angel in Sibford Gower churchyard.*

George and Dragon virtually backs onto the village church and is especially handy for the vicar and his flock, should they be in need of refreshment after a service. The beer is good, and excellent food – ranging from a wholesome sandwich to a substantial meal – is available.

Barton Hill Farm is on the southern edge of Shutford. A public footpath runs south from here to the village of Tadmarton, passing between Jester's Hill and Madmarston Hill, and passing to the west of Upper Lea Farm. A substantial hillfort crowns the top of Madmarston Hill, the earthworks enclosing some seven acres, and several banks and ditches can be seen. The ramparts are best preserved on the north and east sides, however, being in part tree-covered.

This fort has been scientifically examined and dated to the period between the late first century BC and early first century AD. Iron implements, including a blacksmith's poker and an axehead, and a hoard of currency bars, have been found here – all suggesting relative prosperity.

However, returning to road travel, we take a lane north-east out of Shutford, past Wroxton Mill, and join the A422 (Stratford Road) after about a mile and a half. Turning right towards Banbury, we quickly arrive at Wroxton. Soon after joining the A422, however, and immediately before the village, is a lane on the right. This leads to North Newington. Standing on a verge at the junction is an ornate stone direction post, topped with a ball finial. The sign, which was given by one Francis

White in 1686, points out directions to Banbury, London, Stratford and Chipping Norton – each direction indicated by hands that stand proud on the surface of the stone post. About 7ft in height, the sign was restored in the 1970s. The village itself is neat and attractive and has a fine seventeenth-century mansion, Wroxton Abbey, which is on the site of a thirteenth-century priory. In the eighteenth century the architect Sanderson Miller carried out work on the mansion, and is thought to have created an octagonal dovecote, a Gothic arch and an ice-house, which can be seen in the grounds of the abbey. A public footpath runs through the park, past an obelisk, which commemorates a visit by Frederick, Prince of Wales, in 1739.

There are two good pubs in Wroxton. The White Horse stands next to the A422 road in the centre of the village, and The North Arms – a handsome building with a thatched roof and a large garden – is reached by taking a narrow lane, close to The White Horse, down a steep hill into the middle of the village. Both pubs serve good food. Now we take the lane off the A422 – next to the guide post already described – to North Newington, and on to the B4035 road to Broughton – a journey of around two-and-a-half-miles. Broughton is an agreeable little place and has a splendid castle – which started its existence in the early fourteenth century as a fortified manor house, becoming a true castle in 1405. In the sixteenth century the castle was modified, with the removal of most of the battlements. The castle remains little changed since that day and is still in the hands of the Fiennes family – Sir William Fiennes, Lord Saye and Sele, having acquired it in 1451, upon his marriage to the granddaughter of Thomas Wykeham, who had turned the manor house into a castle.

The small church adjoining the castle has much of interest and is full of handsome monuments to members of the Fiennes family. I remember it being used as a location for the Tom Selleck movie *Three Men and a Little Lady* in the late 1980s. On the northern edge of the village I have my own 'secret' place. Actually, it isn't really secret at all, but it's a place I used to visit often with my two infant sons and then-wife in the early 1990s. We used to shop in Banbury quite regularly, and on the return drive to Moreton-in-Marsh, would turn off the main road and park at a lane-side spot near the entrance to Broughton Castle. There, opposite a small meadow occupied by livestock, we would sit munching sandwiches obtained in Banbury. This always seemed to me a timeless little corner of England, with the Sor Brook trickling through the fields next to the parking spot.

To get to Tadmarton, the next 'stop', we continue west on the B4035 road for about a mile and a half. This is a scattered village with a lot of modern development as well as some thatched cottages, and there are pleasant views northwards across rolling green fields. Almost inevitably, there is a pub, The Lampet Arms.

The next village, Swalcliffe, is only about half a mile west. This is a mainly stone-built village with several thatched cottages and an excellent fifteenth-century inn, The Stag's Head, which serves excellent ales and wines, and first class meals. There is a patio and terraced garden, with views over a small stream. The narrow Park Lane runs south from the village to Swalcliffe Grange. At its start it is shaded by woodland and passes some thatched cottages, tucked away in a particularly quiet corner of the village. After passing Swalcliffe Grange we follow the lane across Tadmarton Heath until we arrive at a crossroads – we go straight on here, and also at the next crossroads. The lane by-passes Wigginton and leads into the village of Swerford, almost five miles south of Swalcliffe.

This picturesque little village has a small green, and pretty cottages with roses growing around the doors, and there is a nice church with a thirteenth-century spire.

Close to the church is a Norman motte and bailey, undulations and grassy mounds all over what was obviously the fortified building of someone notable, or a castle used for the control of the local population. The history of the place seems lost in the mists of time, however.

We now head for a real gem of a place, about a mile and a half south-east. From Swerford, drive south for a short distance until you get to the A361 (Banbury Road), and, when you reach it, turn left, then right on to the B4022, which leads into Great Tew. A 'model village' with picturesque stone cottages and a splendid inn The Falkland Arms, Great Tew was constructed in part by the nineteenth-century landscape gardener John Loudon. Lucius Cary, Viscount Falkland, had a manor house here until his death at the Battle of Newbury in 1643. Nothing remains of that building, but the approach to the village church is through a fine seventeenth-century gateway and along a lovely tree-lined path, thought to have originally been the carriageway to Carey's mansion. Both the gateway and walk were restored in 1992. The church walk, and one's first glimpse of the church itself, evokes a feeling of timelessness. I'm no psychic, believe me, but walking along that path in the late 1990s I really felt the 'presence' of a little boy and little girl, dressed in Victorian or Edwardian garb, giggling excitedly as they chased each other. Worryingly, I hadn't even been to The Falkland Arms!

Chipping Norton is about five miles south-west of Great Tew, and is easily reached by following the A361 road. This is a busy little town, active and very much alive. Its market square is overlooked by a fine nineteenth-century town hall and the streets are lined with a number of good shops and welcoming pubs. And though the town does get numerous visitors during the summer, the place is not dominated by the tourist trade. Several of the town's curiosities are on the west side, visible from the A44 road as one travels towards Moreton- in-Marsh. First, down

*The gateway to Church Walk, Great Tew.*

a slope on the left, there is a large, Jacobean-style building with a chimney 165ft tall. It looks a little incongruous in its Cotswold setting and was originally a tweed mill, operated by the Bliss family. Intended to resemble a great house in a park, this fine building was designed by George Woodhouse, an architect from Lancashire. It was built in 1872 and provided employment for some 700 workers, but eventually closed in 1980 after a long decline in business. The old building stood empty for seven years, gradually becoming dilapidated, but in 1989 was converted into a development of luxury flats.

Now heading backing into Chipping Norton, the town cemetery will soon be seen on the left. Visible from the roadside footpath is an unusual memorial in the shape of a five bar gate, and next to this is a substantial headstone bearing an illustration of a horse's head enclosed within a large horseshoe. This is the grave of one Davey Barnard, who died in 1973 aged forty-eight. Local residents have told me that he was a respected local member of the Romany community and that, when he died, his funeral was attended by many people. At the conclusion of the funeral, apparently, his gypsy caravan was burned, as is the custom. The memorial is certainly an elaborate affair and he was obviously held in high regard by those who mourned. On the top bar of the gate there is a poignant message from his wife, Daisy: 'Davey, I love you'.

*The gypsy's grave, Chipping Norton.*

Just after the cemetery the road passes over what was once the railway line from Banbury to Cheltenham. The line closed in 1962, but from the bridge there is a good view of the blocked-up portal of the 685 yard-long Chipping Norton railway tunnel. Then, climbing the hill into the town, New Street on the right leads to the car park, and an ancient stone can be seen on the footpath. No more than a few feet tall, and gnarled and worn by the ravages of time, the stone is visually unimpressive and might easily be overlooked. Situated on an ancient roadway, it is nevertheless of interest and it has been suggested that the stone may once have been a wayside marker to the Rollright Stones, a few miles west.

On into the town centre, then, and a real haven for lovers of the arts will be found in Spring Street. A little theatre, simply called 'The Theatre', has a busy programme of plays, musical concerts and theatrical productions, as well as providing the only cinema for miles around. This is no amateur outfit, either. There are occasional performances by well-known figures from the thespian and musical world, as well as productions by various contemporary companies. The annual Christmas pantomime attracts audiences from all over the district, The Theatre being dubbed by the press as 'the prettiest small theatre in England'. It began life as a disused Salvation Army citadel, which was acquired by two former members of the Royal Shakespeare Company, who recognized the potential for a theatre in the Cotswolds and set about gaining local sponsorship. The project went from strength to strength

*The Hoar Stone, Enstone.*

*Thor's Stone, Taston.*

and professional drama and stage productions are now an established feature of the area. A visit is strongly recommended. There is a pleasant bar in the theatre, but there is also a very good pub, The Chequers, next door – an excellent place for a pre-performance 'livener'.

If we now follow the A44 road east out of town, the A34 will be reached. Turn right, and the village of Enstone will be reached after four miles. This scattered village on the A34 road from Chipping Norton to Oxford is in two halves – Church Enstone and Neat Enstone – that are separated by the River Glyme, which flows through a valley between the two hills. In the seventeenth century a water-engineer named Thomas Bushell fashioned a grotto and 'pleasure-house' near the river. Said to be quite spectacular, it was even visited by King Charles.

There is now no trace of the grotto, nor, sadly, the 'pleasure-house'. In a dense thicket beside the road from Enstone to Spelsbury, however, one can see the Hoar Stone. Dating from about 3500 to 2500 BC, this monument actually consists of three upright stones with three fallen stones in front of them. The tallest of the uprights stands 9ft tall. The remains of the burial chamber of a portal dolmen tomb, the structure would originally have been at the end of a long mound, of which there is now no trace. The surrounding undergrowth lends a rather gaunt and sombre air to the monument and provides an unusual setting.

Taston is a tiny hamlet about a mile and a half south-east of Enstone. Its place-name may possibly have a connection with a heathen shrine – the place is thought to have taken its name from an ancient megalith, which stands awkwardly on a roadside bank next to the lane that runs from Spelsbury to Enstone. The stone, known locally as 'Thor's Stone' or 'Thunor's Stone', is almost 7½ft tall. Curved and gnarled, it is a single monolith with no trace of any other stones in the vicinity, and unlike the Hawk Stone at nearby Spelsbury, does not appear to have ever been part of a barrow. Its date is not known, but it is certainly very ancient. Taston is the only place in the Cotswolds that has a name with heathen origins.

Near the stone is a medieval cross on a base with three steps. The cross itself has long gone, however, only the shaft remaining.

Next to a narrow lane that leads to the B4022 road to Charlbury is a spring of clear water, which flows from an ornate well with a conical turret, before falling into a pool. The water then flows into a pretty stream that runs alongside the lane. In an enchanting setting, the well and pool are on a bank, surrounded by trees that form a delightful glade.

About half a mile to the west is Spelsbury. There is not all that much at this little village overlooking the Evenlode Valley, though it is attractive enough and has a row of gabled seventeenth-century almshouses. There is a Victorian recessed and tile-roofed drinking fountain with seating space, the actual fountain being made of copper in a lion's head sculpture. It was erected about 1900 to the memory of one Constantine Augustus Dillon, the architect believed to be Romaine Walker. Few would describe the fountain as attractive, and in the 1974 volume *The Buildings of England: Oxfordshire*, Jennifer Sherwood and Nikolaus Pevsner amusingly describe it as, 'a hideous shell niche…'

Standing alone in a field about a mile to the north of Spelsbury there is a single standing stone, known as the Hawk Stone, about 7ft tall. In his 1925 book *Long Barrows of the Cotswolds* O.G.S. Crawford describes 'distinct signs of a low mound all round the base of the stone.' It is suspected that this stone may well be the remains of a chambered long barrow.

The next 'stop' on this 'tour' is just over a mile south on the B4026 road. Looking across the Evenlode Valley to Wychwood Forest, the village of Charlbury benefits from being on the Cotswold Line, which runs between Oxford and Worcester. On the station platform are two fine nameplates, painted in the standard Great Western Railway colours of chocolate and cream. These signs pre-date the nationalisation of the railways in 1948.

The village has numerous pleasant cottages and houses, and there are a number of family shops and businesses. At Market Street in the town centre is a traditional pub, The Rose and Crown, which serves a good selection of real ales. Meals are not available, this being a pub for the discerning beer drinker.

Standing on a small green is a stone fountain with eight arched windows, which was designed and built by John Kibble in 1897. A copper plaque on the fountain walls bears the inscription:

THIS FOUNTAIN IS ERECTED TO COMMEMORATE THE VISIT
OF H.M. QUEEN VICTORIA TO CHARLBURY IN NOV 1886,
THE PROVISION OF A WATER SUPPLY FOR THE TOWN IN 1886,
THE 60TH ANNIVERSARY OF THE QUEEN'S ACCESSION
JUNE 20, 1897.

Ascott-under-Wychwood, the next place to be visited, is about four miles west, reached by the B4437 road. This pretty village next to the River Evenlode has the advantage of being situated on the Oxford-Worcester railway line, so, probably more enjoyably, one can take the train – Ascott is only one stop from Charlbury. The village's Norman church is of interest, its chancel arch dating from the thirteenth century. It sits in a large churchyard, full of picturesque tombstones and surrounded on all sides by stone houses.

*The Memorial Fountain in Shipton-under-Wychwood.*

There are earthworks of two castles here: one at the west end of the village known as Ascot Earl is a simple motte-and-bailey construction, the other is the bailey of d'Oyley's castle, built in the twelfth century. This is at Ascott d'Oyley on the north side of the village, where the Manor House stands within the bailey.

Now, here is something of interest to ardent trade unionists: in 1873, following addresses by Joseph Arch, the leader of the National Agricultural Labourers' Union, the village gained brief national notoriety when a strike was begun at a local farm. Following threats made to workers brought in from outside the village, magistrates sentenced sixteen women to a period of hard labour. After an angry crowd had smashed windows at nearby Chipping Norton Police Station, where they were being held, they were taken to Oxford Prison. Even in those rather less enlightened times, the treatment was considered unduly harsh and the Home Secretary subsequently criticised the decision of the magistrates.

Shipton-under-Wychwood is less than a mile west of Ascott, and again, just one stop on the railway line. A scattered village in the valley of the River Evenlode, Shipton-under-Wychwood possesses a number of fine houses and a church with a tall spire, handsome thirteenth-dentury doorway and stone pulpit and font of the fifteenth century. In the churchyard there is a superb three-decker bale tomb to the Morgan family. It is beautifully embellished with intricate carvings of angels, flowers and foliage. Also depicted is an heraldic emblem with what seems to be a lizard.

On the edge of the green is a gabled fountain, erected in 1878 to the memory of seventeen members of the Hedges and Townsend families who set sail to emigrate to New Zealand in 1874. The group set off on the SS *Cospatrick*, but this wooden ship, which had an inflammable cargo, caught fire and sank with the loss of almost 500 people. All seventeen of the Shipton emigrants lost their lives.

Overlooking the green is the fifteenth-century Shaven Crown Hotel, once the haunt of the notorious highwaymen, the Dunsdon brothers. Marginally less odious, the fascist leader Sir Oswald Mosley and his wife Diana – one of the 'Mitford Girls', who died as recently as 2003 – were detained at The Shaven Crown by the authorities during the Second World War. Nowadays the hotel has a rather different class of clientele. The Dunsdon brothers were eventually captured, convicted of murder, and were hanged at Gloucester gaol in 1784 (or was it 1767 or 1785?), before their bodies were taken and hung in chains from a single oak tree some two miles south of Shipton, a little off the A361 road to Fulbrook. Another version of the story is that they were taken, still alive, and hanged in chains in the tree, where they remained until they rotted. They carved their initials and the date into the bark of the tree, it is claimed, the tree becoming known as 'The Gibbet Tree'. Certainly Mollie Harris, writer, broadcaster and former member of *The Archers* cast, makes mention in her 1989 book *Where The Windrush Flows* of seeing the initials there.

Burford, unfortunately, is not on the railway line. About three miles south-west of Shipton-under-Wychwood, it is reached by the A361 road. The main street through Burford surely rivals that of Chipping Campden as one of the prettiest in the Cotswolds. Running up a hill from where its medieval bridge crosses the River Windrush, it is lined with a variety of fine houses. Near the main car park, and of special interest, is the town's ancient Church of St John the Baptist, which dates in part from the twelfth century, and has many architectural features of note. A sculptured stone slab has been built into the south wall of the internal turret. It shows three figures – one mounted, two on foot – whose identity is unknown. A remnant of an early pagan culture, the carving probably dates from about 160 *AD*.

Outside the church the Romanesque west door dating from about 1175 has striking zig-zag mouldings and a row of carvings, sadly disfigured by weather. The door itself and its iron hinges are probably original. In the churchyard near this door is a large Roman coffin of stone, weighing three-quarters of a ton. It was found in 1814 near the River Windrush at nearby Taynton.

*The war memorial, Westwell.*

Also of interest is the font, which bears a curious inscription. In 1649 at Salisbury there had been a mutiny of 'Levellers' – radicals who believed that Cromwell was betraying their hard-won cause. They marched towards Banbury to join other disaffected soldiers, but were captured in Burford by Cromwell and Fairfax. About 340 of them were locked up in Burford church, though many escaped. While being held, one of the men scratched his name into the lead lining of the font: 'Anthony Sedley, prisner, 1649'. This can still be seen on the south side, under the glass cover. The prisoners were forced to watch as the four ringleaders were taken outside and shot, but soon after, those remaining were given a pardon by Cromwell.

Visitors are well catered for in the town. There are various welcoming inns, hotels and cafés, and there are numerous shops offering a range of wares. Burford has a busy, but welcoming air about it, and one can easily spend several hours here.

The next village, a couple of miles south-west of the bustle of Burford, is, I think, among the most serene in the Cotswolds – and yet the A40 to Oxford and Cheltenham is easily reached. Very small and unspoilt, Westwell has a Norman church with several seventeenth- and eighteenth-century table tombs in the churchyard, and close to the village pond and green is a particularly striking monument. The war memorial, in commemoration of two brothers who died in the First World War, consists of a great block of rough-hewn stone on two steps. A brass figure 'I', rescued from the clock on the ruined Cloth Hall at Ypres, is set into the stone, a poignant reminder of that awful conflict. Standing like a sentinel, this unusual war memorial appears almost eerie in such gentle surroundings.

Now, I am afraid, we must endure one of my famous 'treks' again. Kelmscot, our next destination, is worth the effort, though. Take the lane south-east from Westwell, past Holwell and the perimeters of the Cotswold Wildlife Park, until the A361 road is reached. Head south towards Lechlade, then after a few miles, take a road on the left towards Little Faringdon. Drive through Little Faringdon and on until the B4449 road is reached, just outside Kelmscot. This small village to the north of the Thames is notable as the home of social reformer, poet, painter, architect and craftsman William Morris from 1871 until his death in 1896. He lived at the Elizabethan Kelmscot Manor, set on the banks of the Thames, which he bought in partnership with his friend Rossetti. Filled with his works, as well as pictures by his friends Rossetti and Burne-Jones, it is only open to the public from the beginning of April until the end of September.

Kelmscot's Memorial Cottages, erected by Jane Morris in memory of her husband, bear a stone carving of Morris sitting beneath trees, and in the churchyard is his tomb, designed by Philip Webb.

In the middle of this tranquil stone village there is an inviting hostelry, The Plough Inn, with the base of a medieval village cross situated on grass to the front of the building.

Having almost reached Wiltshire, we will now head north once again. First we return to Burford via the A361 – about nine miles – then we follow the B4425 east out of Burford, above the meandering River Windrush. About a mile and a half east of the town is a little place named Widford, our next 'stop'. There is very little at this tiny hamlet above the Windrush Valley. A sixteenth- and seventeenth-century manor house is attractive, but the most interesting feature is the little Church of Saint Oswald, a thirteenth-century building built upon the site of a Roman villa. A small section of mosaic floor has been preserved and is visible in the centre of the building. Quite apart from the mosaic, the church is of interest. There are flag-stone floors, fourteenth-century wall paintings, a Jacobean pulpit and nineteenth-century box pews. All this lends the church a delightfully unspoiled appearance.

Continuing east from Widford, we arrive at Swinbrook after less than a mile. A lovely village, Swinbrook has a church that is full of interest. There are various grand wall monuments, including two three-decker monuments with effigies of members of the Fettiplace family. Fragments of medieval glass can be identified in the east window of the south aisle, collected in 1940 after a German landmine exploded in the village and blew the east window out. In the churchyard there are several fine bale tombs. The Fettiplaces once owned a great mansion near the church, but this was demolished in 1805. The only visible remnant of any interest is a medieval fish pond.

After his father fell at Ypres in the First World War, Captain the Hon. David Mitford inherited the title of Lord Redesdale. He inherited Batsford Estate at Moreton-in-Marsh from his cousin, the Earl of Redesdale, then, at the end of the war, moved to Asthall Manor and then to nearby Swinbrook. His daughters were the four famous Mitford girls, and in Swinbrook churchyard will be found the plain modern graves of Nancy, the novelist, and her sister, Unity.

Asthall is less than a mile east of Swinbrook. This little stone village is a treat. Close to the River Windrush and on the course of the Roman Akeman Street, Asthall was the home of the Mitford family in the 1930s, after they moved from Batsford, near Moreton-in-Marsh. They lived at the Elizabethan manor for six years, before moving to nearby Swinbrook.

The church is partly Norman, and has been somewhat over-restored. The medieval glass in the Cornwall Chapel windows is worth seeing, though, as are the churchyard's seventeenth- and eighteenth-century tombs.

Also in the village is an interesting and easily overlooked example of wartime graffiti. Carved into the parapet of the three-arched bridge over the River Windrush is a Lee Enfield rifle. The river is very picturesque here and there are pleasant walks from the bridge – west towards Swinbrook and east towards Minster Lovell – and close by the footpath there is space on the roadside for the parking of a couple of vehicles. A charming hostelry, The Maytime Inn, is situated in the centre of the village.

To get to Minster Lovell, the next place of interest, we need to take the lane south out of Asthall, which joins the B4047 road to Witney. This takes us directly to Minster Lovell, about three miles east. This village has cottages of stone and thatch, and there is a nicely appointed hotel called The Old Swan. There is a very interesting fifteenth-century church, too, with fine vaulting and a knight's tomb. The most outstanding feature of the village, however, is the ruined fifteenth-century Minster Lovell Hall. This manor belonged to the Lovell family from the twelfth century, though the house whose ruins are seen today was built about 1431-42 by William, the seventh Lord Lovell, who incorporated parts of an earlier building. Much folklore surrounds the ruin, and the 'mistletoe bough' story, in which a young bride dies, trapped in an attic chest after concealing herself too effectively in a game of hide-and-seek, is attributed to this house.

The haunting ruins stand in a beautiful setting, with the River Windrush flowing close by, and are among the most attractive ruined monuments in the Cotswolds.

Now, having explored the most interesting villages along this stretch of Oxfordshire's Cotswolds, we have to return north once again. The little village of Idbury is about nine miles north-west of Minster Lovell. It is suggested that the lane north out of Minster Lovell be followed over the River Windrush and on through the hamlets of Asthall Leigh and Fordwells, before arriving at the southern outskirts of Shipton-under-Wychwood. A lane then passes south of Milton-under-Wychwood and through Fifield, until it arrives at Idbury. From Idbury there are lovely views over the Evenlode Valley to the Oxfordshire Cotswolds and, though the village is very small, there are a couple of curiosities. The Tudor manor house was the home of J.W. Robertson Scott, founder of *The Countryman* magazine, from 1922. The Manor House was the editorial office of the magazine until it moved to Burford in the late 1940s and a tablet over the door is inscribed 'Oh more than happy countryman, if he but knew his good fortune'.

Idbury church, with nineteenth-century box pews and a fine octagonal font, is particularly appealing. In the churchyard is the tomb of notable engineer, Sir Benjamin Baker, one of the two great engineers of the Forth Railway Bridge, which was completed in 1890. In 1907 an obituary in *The Times* said that the bridge 'owes its inception in its present form to Sir Benjamin Baker'. Baker was also involved with the building of Victoria Station and was consulting engineer for the first Aswan dam. The grave has four flying buttresses surmounted by a Celtic cross and is the most elaborate structure in what is quite a small churchyard. Curiously, Baker was not from Idbury, but had specially requested that he be buried here.

Kingham, the next 'stop', is about three miles north-east of Idbury. The railway line from Worcester to Oxford – and subsequently on to London – passes through the village, close to the border with Gloucestershire. The station, though very welcome in the area, is a relatively plain modern building. As at nearby Charlbury, the platform signs indicating the station's name are, however, much older. They are painted in the standard Great Western Railway colours of chocolate and cream and are more than fifty years old, pre-dating the nationalisation of the railway in 1948.

The village has a welcoming hostelry, The Tollgate Inn, and a useful post office and village store. A large block of rough-hewn stone about 5ft high stands on the triangular village green as a memorial to the men and women who served in the conflicts of the twentieth century.

A pleasant walk can be taken from the railway station to the neighbouring village of Bledington. This involves crossing a small bridge over a large stream off the River Evenlode. Beneath the bridge the water becomes a waterfall, but do not expect a cascade to rival the Niagra Falls. The waterfall is actually very modest, but even so, is a rarity in the North Cotswolds and surely merits an appreciative glance. A few

*The ruins of the fifteenth-century Minster Lovell Hall.*

*Benjamin Baker's grave, Idbury.*

*The old signal box, Bruern.*

*The long barrow, Lyneham.*

yards on towards Bledington (which is actually in Gloucestershire), and the road crosses the River Evenlode where it passes an old mill. Again, this is a welcome sight and is the last scenic spot until one actually arrives in Bledington – where there is a village shop and post office, and a pleasant pub, The King's Head. Running through the village is a pretty stream, much used by mallards and moorhens.

There is very little to see at the hamlet of Bruern, about two-and-a-half miles south of Kingham. A Cistercian abbey was founded here around 1137, but it was sold soon after the Dissolution in 1539, and no traces remain. The present mansion that stands close to the original monastic site by the River Evenlode was built about 1720.

The Cotswold railway line from Oxford to Worcester passes the edge of the hamlet, the road from Sarsden to Fifield crossing the line near the abbey site. On the approach of a train the road traffic is controlled by automatic crossing barriers, which replaced the wooden signal box when it was closed and removed in 1974. The disused signal box now stands in the garden of a cottage about 100 yards from the line, providing a striking roadside curiosity.

Lyneham village is just over half a mile from Bruern, but its most interesting feature is another couple of miles away, next to the A361 road to Chipping Norton. This is the remains of a long barrow, which measures 170ft long, with a single upright stone 6ft high standing at the north end. This may be the remains of a blind entrance. The barrow was excavated late in the nineteenth century, with two burial chambers, apparently of the lateral type, being revealed. G.E. Daniel, however, in his

*One of the two stone gate pillars beside the road near Sarsden.*

*Prehistoric Chamber Tombs of England and Wales* expressed the view that the monument consisted of 'a number of cists with a single standing stone'. Human and animal bones were found during the dig, as well as two Saxon burials. The mound is much overgrown with trees and bramble bushes, but the single upright stone is very accessible and easy to see. The barrow dates from about 3500–2500 BC.

Just under two miles north-west of Lyneham long barrow is the small hamlet of Sarsden. Situated in wooded parkland, it has a few cottages and a splendid seventeenth-century mansion, landscaped by Humphrey Repton. The remnants of a medieval cross, consisting of the shaft on a large polygonal base with five steps, can be seen near a crossroads on the road between Churchill and Chadlington. A mile to the east, on the large roadside verge of the A361 road, are two impressive eighteenth-century pillars, with large ball finials. Not obviously denoting any territory or entrance, the tall pillars look rather ingongruous. They are thought to be connected with nearby Sarsden House.

It is only about half a mile from Sarsden to Churchill. This village has a handsome nineteenth-century church, its west tower a copy of the tower of Magdalen College, Oxford. All that is left of the original church is the chancel, now used as a mortuary chapel.

Prominent at the crossroads in the centre of the village is a substantial block of weathered local stone, which stands as a striking monument to William Smith –

*The William Smith monument in Churchill.*

'Father of British Geology'. A son of the village blacksmith, he was born at Churchill on 23 March 1769 before going on to become an engineer and canal builder and, subsequently, a pioneer geologist. Smith's most important discovery was the importance of fossils in determining the ages of rock strata. He died at Northampton on 28 August 1839, the monolith being erected by the Earl of Ducie in 1891.

Surprisingly, for such a small place, Churchill has produced two great men. Warren Hastings, who became Governor-General of India and was largely responsible for establishing the British Empire in India in the eighteenth century, was born in a house between the two churches.

Another curious feature in Churchill is its large drinking fountain. Of somewhat bizarre appearance, it consists of a square tower with obelisks and flying buttresses, and a short spire. It was constructed in 1870 as a memorial to James Langston, who had paid for the building of the new church, and had improved the agriculture of the village. Never ones to mince their words, Jennifer Sherwood and Nikolaus Pevsner describe the fountain as 'memorably ugly' in *The Buildings Of England: Oxfordshire*.

In the centre of the village is an excellent place at which to enjoy a drink and a meal. For many years the village pub, The Chequers, was closed, but has now been re-opened – quickly gaining a good reputation for fine food and excellent service.

And now, after travelling for many miles, and into four counties, we drive the two-and-a-half miles north-west to Cornwell, near the A436 road to Stow-on-

*Crawford's 'barrow circle'.*

the-Wold. This is a truly lovely village, which in the late 1930s was bought by a wealthy American lady. At that time the estate was in poor condition and the lady engaged architect Clough Williams-Ellis to restore it. His most famous work is at Portmeirion in North Wales and there are some reflections of that highly personal style to be seen in Cornwell.

Roughly a mile north of the village are what seem to be the remnants of a mysterious ancient monument. In his 1925 book *Long Barrows of the Cotswolds* O.G.S. Crawford mentions finding a quantity of large stones on the ridge between Adlestrop and the Rollright Stones. These he considered to be the remains of a 'barrow-circle', not shown on any map. Apparently, the stones were mentioned by Sir Arthur Evans in 1895 in a folklore article about the Rollright Stones. I have visited a spot in a field just off the A436 road a few hundred yards south-west of its junction with the A44 near the Cross Hands public house and found two stones lying prostrate within a wooded area. One, measuring about 5ft square, might possibly be the remains of a portal dolmen. Another stone nearby measured about 6ft by 3ft. In a clump of trees close by a number of prostrate large stones were seen, some over 9ft in length. On the north-eastern side of the trees a mound of rough stones was observed, apparently haphazardly piled. Whether they were in their original position must be open to conjecture, however cairns are shown in this position on the 1951 Ordnance Survey map, and on the more recent 1983 edition a tumulus is indicated. The main group of stones did appear to form one side of a circle, though again it could not be stated that they were in their original positions. Expert opinion is needed to try and ascertain whether this is indeed Crawford's 'barrow-circle'

And so, then, we have completed my journey around the Cotswolds. This truly is a lovely area and I hope that you have gained pleasure from its towns, villages, hills and meadows. The reader is forgiven if he or she assumes that I really did have a 'Bobby's job'. Few can fail to have observed that mine was a gentle kind of policing, and that I don't seem to have gone without the pleasures of hearty ales and companionable ladies. It is indeed true that my time as a Cotswolds policeman was, in the main, very enjoyable. Actually, I often think I was lucky enough to catch the last years of a rather old-fashioned policing style – a style of 'village bobbying' that has now gone forever.

There were some unwelcome moments, of course – no one spends twenty-odd years as a policeman without seeing a certain amount of unpleasantness – but these were the exceptions, rather than the rule. In the interests of humour and a light read I have chosen to depict Cotswolds-style policing as, perhaps, slightly incompetent, but most of my colleagues were actually thoroughly professional officers, who displayed integrity, common sense and sound judgement. I hope that they will remember how fortunate they were to have worked in Gloucestershire's Cotswolds.

# GLOSSARY

| | |
|---|---|
| arcade: | series of arches supported on columns |
| capital: | top part of a column |
| castellated: | decorated with defensive battlements |
| capstone: | roofing stone to burial chamber |
| chancel: | where the altar is placed, in the east end of the church |
| corbel: | block of stone projecting from a wall, with a feature supported on its level surface |
| cupola: | small domed turret crowning a roof |
| dolmen: | tomb in the form of a large flat stone laid on upright stones |
| Doric: | ancient order – Greek, Roman etc. |
| effigy: | figure representing image |
| gable: | triangular upper part of wall at end of roof |
| gazebo: | raised summer house or look-out tower |
| lintel: | horizontal stone or timber over door, window or aperture |
| lynchet: | terraced strip on sloping fields caused by soil creep from ploughing along – rather than against – hillside |
| megalith: | term applied to burial chambers made of large stones |
| motte: | mound forming the site of eleventh- and twelfth-century castles |
| nave | main body of church building, from west door to chancel |
| ogee: | a style of arch especially popular in the fourteenth century |
| parapet: | low wall placed to protect against sudden drop – bridge, housetop, etc. |

| | |
|---|---|
| Perpendicular: | English Gothic architecture of the fifteenth and sixteenth centuries |
| pinnacle: | ornamental turret, usually conical or in shape of pyramid, crowning tower, roof, buttress |
| portal: | doorway, often elaborate |
| pulpit: | raised platform in church, from which the preacher delivers a sermon |
| quoins: | dressed stones at the angles of a building |
| rood: | cross or crucifix |
| transept: | transverse part of a cross-shaped church |
| trefoil: | three-lobed ornamentation |
| tympanum: | space between the lintel of a doorway and the arch above it |

# BIBLIOGRAPHY

BAGUST, Harold – Stow-on-the-Wold – Aztec Publishing (1979)

BECKINSALE, R.P. – Companion Into Gloucestershire – Methuen (1939)

BECKWITH, E.G.C. – What To See In Historical Blockley – Beckwith (1980)

BICK, D.E. – Old Leckhampton – Bick

BOWYER, Michael J.F. – Action Stations: Military airfields of the Cotswolds and the Central Midlands – Patrick Stephens Limited (1983)

BRILL, Edith – Portrait of the Cotswolds – Hale (1964)

BRILL, Edith – Cotswold Ways – Hale (1985)

BRILL, Edith and TURNER, Peter – The Minor Pleasures of Cotswold – Dent (1971)

BRYSON, Bill – Notes From A Small Island – Doubleday (1995)

CAUDLE, Everard – Light On Leckhampton

COPE, Julian – The Modern Antiquarian – Thorsons (1998)

CRAWFORD, O.G.S. – Long Barrows of the Cotswolds – John Bellows (1925)

DANIEL, G.E. – The Prehistoric Chamber Tombs of England and Wales – Cambridge University Press (1950)

DARVILL, Timothy – Prehistoric Gloucestershire – Alan Sutton and Gloucestershire County Library (1987)

DIXON, Reginald – Cotswold Curiosities – The Dovecote Press Ltd (1988)

DRINKWATER, P. – Mediaeval Chapels of the Stour Valley – Drinkwater (1983)

DRINKWATER, P. – Ways And Waymarks in the Four Shires – Drinkwater (1980)

DUCKWORTH, Francis – The Cotswolds – Adam and Charles Black (1908)

FIGGURES, Molly – Over the Bones – Drinkwater (1978)

FINBERG, H.P.R. – Gloucestershire – Hodder & Stoughton Ltd. (1955)

FINBERG, Josceline – The Cotswolds – Methuen (1977)

GLOUCESTERSHIRE FEDERATION OF WOMEN'S INSTITUTES – The Gloucestershire Village Book – Countryside Books/GFWI (1987)

HADFIELD, Charles and NORRIS, John – Waterways to Stratford – David & Charles (1962)

HADFIELD, Charles and Mary – The Cotswolds – Batsford (1966)

HADFIELD, Charles and Alice Mary – Introducing the Cotswolds – David & Charles (1976)

HAMLIN, John F. and TYACK, Gerry V. – Royal Air Force Moreton-in-Marsh – A History – Tyack (1995)

HANDLEY, B.M. and DINGWALL, R. – The Wye Valley Railway and the Coleford Branch – The Oakwood Press (1998)

HARRIS, Mollie – Where the Windrush Flows – Alan Sutton (1989)

HARRIS, Mollie – Wychwood: The Secret Cotswold Forest – Alan Sutton (1991)

HAWKES, Jacquetta – Prehistoric and Roman Monuments in England and Wales – Chatto & Windus (1951)

HEIGHWAY, Carolyn – Anglo-Saxon Gloucestershire – Alan Sutton and Gloucestershire County Library (1987)

HORDE, T. – The Muse in Gloucestershire – (1800)

ICELY, H.E.M. – Blockley Through Twelve Centuries

JENKINS, S.C. and CARPENTER, R.S. – The Shipston-on-Stour Branch – Wild Swan Publications (1997)

JOHNSON, Joan – The Gloucestershire Gentry – Alan Sutton (1989)

JOHNSON, Joan – Stow-on-the-Wold – Alan Sutton (1980)

JOHNSON, Joan – A Short History of Moreton-in-Marsh – Four Shire Books (1996)

McCORMICK, Donald – Murder By Witchcraft – John Long (1968)

McWHIRR, Alan – Roman Gloucestershire – Alan Sutton (1981)

MAGGS, Colin – Railways of The Cotswolds – Peter Nicholson (1981)

MEADES, Eileen – The History of Chipping Norton – Bodkin Bookshop (1984)

MEE, Arthur – The King's England: Gloucestershire – Hodder & Stoughton (1938)

MEE, Arthur – The King's England: Oxfordshire – Hodder & Stoughton (1942)

MEE, Arthur – The King's England: Warwickshire – Hodder & Stoughton (1936)

MEE, Arthur – The King's England: Worcestershire – Hodder & Stoughton (1938)

MORETON-IN-MARSH & DISTRICT LOCAL HISTORY SOCIETY – Four Shire Memories – (1992)

MORETON-IN-MARSH & DISTRICT LOCAL HISTORY SOCIETY – Memories of Moreton – Drinkwater (1989)

MOORE, Ann – Curiosities of Worcestershire – S.B. Publications (1991)

NORRIS, John – The Stratford & Moreton Tramway – Railway & Canal Historical Society (1987)

OAKLEY, Mike – Gloucestershire Railway Stations – The Dovecote Press (2003)

PEVSNER, Nikolaus, & WEDGWOOD, Alexandra – The Buildings of England: Warwickshire – Penguin (1966)

PEVSNER, Nikolaus – The Buildings of England: Worcestershire – Penguin (1968)

PIGRAM, Ron and EDWARDS, Dennis F. – Cotswold Memories – Unicorn Books (1990)

POWELL, Geoffrey – The Book Of Campden – Barracuda Books Limited (1982)

PROTZ, Roger (Ed) – Good Beer Guide – Camra Books (2004)

RAINSBERRY, Edward – Through The Lych Gate – The Roundwood Press (1969)

RENNISON, John – Wings Over Gloucestershire – Piccadilly Publishing (1988)

RICHARDSON, L. – Wells and Springs of Gloucestershire – HMSO (1930)

ROLT, L.T.C. – Red For Danger – The Bodley Head Limited (1955)

RUSSELL, J.H. – The Banbury and Cheltenham Railway – Oxford Publishing Co. (1977)

RYDER, T.A. – Portrait Of Gloucestershire – Robert Hale (1966)

SEYMOUR, Aubrey – The Land Where I Belong – The Roundwood Press (1968)

SEYMOUR, Aubrey – Fragrant The Fertile Earth – The Roundwood Press (1970)

SEYMOUR, Aubrey – A Square Mile of Old England- The Roundwood Press (1972)

SHERWOOD, Jennifer and PEVSNER, Nikolaus – The Buildings Of England: Oxfordshire – Penguin (1974)

SKYRING WALTERS, R.C. – Ancient Wells, Springs and Holy Wells Of Gloucestershire – St Stephen's Press (1928)

SMITH, Brian – The Cotswolds – Batsford (1976)

SOLLARS, Margaret – Hidden Gloucestershire – Countryside Books (1988)

SULLIVAN D.P. – Old Stones of Gloucestershire – Reardon & Son (1991)

THOMAS, Nicholas – Guide to Prehistoric England – Batsford (1976)

TIMPSON, John – Timpson's Towns of England and Wales  Jarrold (1989)

TITCHMARSH, Peter and Helen – The Cotswolds – Jarrold (1989)

TURNER, Mark – Folklore and Mysteries of the Cotswolds – Hale (1993)

UNIVERSITY OF LONDON INSTITUTE OF HISTORICAL RESEARCH – The Victoria History of the County of Gloucester – Oxford University Press (1965)

VEREY, David – The Buildings of England – Gloucestershire: The Cotswolds – Penguin (1970)

VEREY, David – Cotswold Churches – Batsford Limited – (1976)

VINER, David – The Thames and Severn Canal – Tempus – (2002)

WARNE, Rev. W.L. – A Short History of Moreton-in-Marsh – The Journal Press (1948)

WHITEMAN, Robin and TALBOT, Rob – The Cotswolds – Weidenfeld & Nicolson (1987)

WHITFIELD, Christopher – A History of Chipping Campden – Shakespeare Head Press (1958)

WHITINGTON-EGAN, Richard – The Great British Torso Mystery – The Bluecoat Press (2002)

WOOD, Eric S. – Field Guide to Archaeology In Britain – Collins (1968)

WRIGHT, Geoffrey N. – The Cotswolds – David & Charles (1991)

In addition to those publications listed above, various issues of the following newspapers, magazines, journals and periodicals have been consulted:

*Cotswold Journal*
*Cotswold Life*
*Gloucestershire Echo*
*Gloucestershire and Wiltshire Standard*
*The Independent*
*The Observer*
*The Times*
*Transactions of the Bristol and Gloucestershire Archaeological Society*

# Index

If you are interested in purchasing other books published by Tempus,
or in case you have difficulty finding any Tempus books in your local bookshop,
you can also place orders directly through our website

**www.tempus-publishing.com**